From Unread to Misread

*Hebrews
to
Revelation*

Neglected New Testament Books

Doug Rowston

Published by
GRACE & PEACE BOOKS
4A Wurilba Ave Hawthorn SA 5062 Australia
djrowston@gmail.com

© 2021 Douglas James Rowston

All rights reserved. This publication is copyright. Other than for the purposes of and subject to the conditions of the Copyright Act, no part of it may in any form or by any means (electronic, mechanical, microcopying, photocopying, recording or otherwise) be reproduced, stored in a retrieval system or transmitted without prior written permission from the publisher.

First printed November 2021

ISBN 978-0-6453288-0-6

Acknowledgements

The front cover is a mosaic of *The Tree of Life* made by my sister Carol Treadwell. The Tree of Life is mentioned at the beginning and end of the Bible as the symbol of God's gift of life to the faithful.

Bible quotations are from the New Revised Standard Version Bible, Anglicized Edition, copyright © 1989, 1995 by the Division of Christian Education of the National Council of Churches of Christ in the U S A. Used by permission. All rights reserved.

This book is dedicated to Church Ministers, School Teachers, and Theological Lecturers in Melbourne, Louisville, and Adelaide who have helped me grow in the grace and knowledge of our Lord and Saviour Jesus Christ.

Blessed Lord, who caused all holy Scriptures to be written for our learning: help us so to hear them, to read, mark, learn, and inwardly digest them, that, through patience, and the comfort of your holy word, we may embrace and for ever hold fast the hope of everlasting life which you have given us in our Saviour Jesus Christ. Amen.

Thomas Cranmer (1489-1556)

CONTENTS

Introduction	1
1 The World of the New Testament	5
2 The Letter to the Hebrews	17
3 The Letter of James	31
4 The First Letter of Peter	39
5 The Letter of Jude & the Second Letter of Peter	49
6 The Three Letters of John	71
7 The Book of Revelation	83
8 Conclusion	95
Annotated Bibliography	97

Introduction

I invite my readers to travel from the Unread (Hebrews) to the Misread (Revelation) in the following pages. This book has been written after I taught a couple of courses at St Barnabas College, Adelaide. One of the courses was entitled 'Alternative New Testament Voices.' It included the books from Hebrews to Jude. The other was called 'The Johannine Literature.' It encompassed the Gospel and Letters of John as well as the Revelation to John. The task of teaching adult students about these New Testament writings always proves to be most enjoyable.

In the process I have drawn upon the wisdom of a range of scholars. My favourites of yesteryear include George Beasley-Murray, Raymond Brown, and F.F. Bruce. Among recent admired authors are Alan Culpepper, James Dunn, and N.T. Wright. I have also directed students to contributions to *The New Interpreter's Bible* and *The New Interpreter's Dictionary of the Bible*. Of course, select bibliographies are attached to each chapter.

But above all, students are encouraged to read the New Testament books themselves. Such modern translations as *New Revised Standard Version, Revised English Bible, New International Version*, and *English Standard Version* are worth reading side by side. The advanced student can tackle *The UBS Greek New Testament*. The beginner can refer to *Good News Bible* which is ideal for English as Second Language readers.

The first chapter is about the world of the New Testament. To read these neglected books requires an understanding of the history of the times.

Then the succeeding chapters will make sense of the time and place of the writing of each document. A similar pattern is followed as documents are examined:

(1) Message — What is the content of the document/s?
(2) Milieu & Meaning — What are the time & place of writing, the purpose & reason for writing?
(3) Mission — What is the significance then and now in the witness of the church?

The second chapter is about the Letter to the Hebrews written in the 60s or the 80s perhaps from Rome. The third chapter deals with the Letter of James composed in the 70s or 90s probably to Christians outside Palestine. The fourth chapter introduces the First Letter of Peter written by a secretary of Peter in the 60s during the time of Nero or a disciple of Peter between 70 and 90 to Christians in the north of Asia Minor. The fifth chapter is about the Letter of Jude and the Second Letter of Peter. The former may have been written in the 90s from Palestine and the latter may be dated in the decades after Jude perhaps from Rome. The sixth chapter covers the Three Letters of John to Christians in a community at Ephesus after the Gospel of John about 100. Finally, the seventh chapter tackles Revelation probably written from Patmos to Christians in the west of Asia Minor during the time of Domitian.

The real meaning of these books in the New Testament is for us to meet Jesus. He is spoken of as *the pioneer and perfecter of our faith* (Hebrews), *our glorious Lord Jesus Christ* (James), *the shepherd and guardian of your souls* (1 Peter), *our only Master and Lord* (Jude), *our Lord and Saviour* (2 Peter), *the true God* (1 John), and *the Alpha and the Omega, the first and the last* (Revelation).

These New Testament books are a means to an end. There is a difference between looking at the window of the New Testament and looking through the window of the New Testament to the world beyond.

Doug Rowston

Parthenon, Athens

Forum, Rome

1 The World of the NT
Jewish hope, Greek language, Roman peace

An Overview of the History of NT Times
A Succession of Rulers:
   Greeks
   Ptolemies
   Seleucids
   Hasmoneans
   Romans
   Herods
   Governors
A Succession of Revolts:
   The First Jewish Revolt
   Separation of Jews and Christians
   The Second Jewish Revolt
The Roman World:
   Competing Faiths
   Alternative Philosophies
   A Hostile State

The Greeks

The Greeks became rulers of the middle east under Alexander the Great (356-323 BC). In 336 BC, Alexander became the ruler of Greece. In 332 BC, he became the ruler of Palestine. In 331 BC, he became the ruler of Persia. Alexander not only extended his empire but he also spread the Greek way of life. This had five features. First, the gymnasium was the training centre for athletic fitness of Greek men. Second, the guild of young men aged 18 wore the broad brimmed Greek hat. Third, the sports stadium featured wrestling, discus throwing, and horse racing. Fourth, the theatre gave Greek entertainment in the form of plays, both tragedy and comedy. Fifth, the Greek language was the simplified common language of the known world.

Palestine's Rulers

After Alexander's death in 323 BC, his kingdom was divided into three parts (Macedon, Asia, and Egypt). Before the coming of the Romans in 63 BC, Palestine was ruled by the Ptolemies of Alexandria in Egypt from 320 to 198 BC, and by the Seleucids of Antioch in Syria from 198 to 142 BC. Between 142 and 63 BC. the Hasmoneans of Judea were the rulers of the Jews.

The Ptolemies

During the Ptolemaic period three features of Jewish life became significant. First, the Dispersion consisted of many Jewish communities scattered throughout the Greek world, yet part of the life of the Greek cities. Second, the Synagogue was the meeting place of Jews in the Greek towns for worship and education. Third, the Septuagint was the Greek translation of the Hebrew Old Testament for the benefit of the Greek speaking Jews.

The Seleucids

During the Seleucid period the Jews revolted against the Syrian King Antiochus IV. He called himself Antiochus Epiphanes ('God Manifest') but the Jews called him Antiochus Epimanes ('Mad Man'). The Maccabean Revolt began in 167 BC under the leadership of Mattathias, and then, his son Judas the Maccabee ('Hammer'). It ended successfully in 164 BC with a

Feast of Dedication. In 167 BC Antiochus IV had defiled the Temple in Jerusalem by setting up a pagan image and by sacrificing a pig on the altar. This was *the abomination of desolation* mentioned in the book of Daniel and the first book of Maccabees. It was the task of the Maccabees of the House of Hashmon to cleanse the sanctuary and dedicate it afresh to the Lord in 164 BC.

The Hasmoneans

Complete independence was gained from the Syrians by Simon, a brother of Judas the Maccabee, in 142 BC. Between 142 and 63 BC the Hasmonean family provided the rulers of the Jewish state. Civil war in Judea from 67 to 63 BC allowed the Romans under Pompey to take control and thereby to bring the independence of the Hasmonean rulers to an end.

The Hasmonean Dynasty

Judas	165-160 BC
Jonathan	160-142 BC
Simon	142-134 BC
John Hyrcanus I	134-104 BC
Aristobulus I	104-103 BC
Alexander Janneus	103-76 BC
Alexandra	76-67 BC
Aristobulus II	67-63 BC
Hyrcanus II	63-40 BC
Antigonus	40-37 BC

Three Influential Groups

During the Hasmonean period three parties came to the fore in Jewish life. First were the Pharisees, nationalistic laymen numbering 6000 in the time of Jesus, who valued the law of Moses interpreted by reference to an inherited tradition. Second were the Sadducees, priests or landowners, who rejected any additions to the law of Moses, set great store by the Temple and its ritual, and so were religious conservatives and political liberals. Third were the Essenes, ascetics numbering 4000 in the time of Jesus, who awaited the coming of the last days in isolated communities such as Qumran near the Dead Sea. About half a million Jews lived alongside a million non-Jews in first century Palestine. Most of the 50,000 people in and around Jerusalem were Jewish.

The Romans

The Romans took advantage of civil war in Judea and Pompey captured Jerusalem in 63 BC. Herod Antipater, an Idumaean, was the man in whom the Romans vested power. He curried favour with Pompey until Pompey's death and then with Julius Caesar until Caesar's assassination. Antipater himself was murdered in 43 BC. His successor was his son Herod the Great who also supported the most powerful Roman politician. His allegiance to Mark Antony lasted until Octavian replaced Antony as ruler. His allegiance to Octavian resulted in the granting of Cleopatra's Palestinian territories to his care.

Herod the Great

Herod the Great ruled as the king of the Jews appointed by the Romans from 37 to 4 BC. His aim was to keep Judea intact and prosperous with the co-operation and protection of Rome. He embarked on a large scale building programme in Jerusalem, Jericho, Samaria, Caesarea, and Masada. Herod hoped to win Jewish acceptance by rebuilding and beautifying the second temple of Zerubbabel. The project begun in 20 BC was not completed until AD 63. Herod failed to win public acceptance before his death in 4 BC. His many purges of real or imagined rivals, his polygamous and adulterous relationships, his repression of any messianic movement (as in Matthew 2:1-18), his alienation of Pharisees and Essenes, and his lack of racial purity - all these things were against him. On his death his kingdom was divided by Augustus (formerly known as Octavian) among three of his sons.

The Sons of Herod

Herod Antipas ruled Galilee and Perea from 4 BC to AD 39. He built the city of Tiberias. In Matthew 14:1-12 and Mark 6:14-29 reference is made to his illegal marriage to his niece and sister-in-law Herodias and to his callous execution of John the Baptist. In Luke 23:6-12 Antipas meets Jesus who is on trial for his life. (According to Luke 13:32 Jesus had previously called Antipas a fox.) Jesus' unwillingness to perform a miracle leads to Antipas' mocking treatment of Jesus. Philip ruled Ituraea and Trachonitis from 4 BC to AD 34. He built the cities of Caesarea Philippi and Bethsaida. Philip is mentioned with Antipas in Luke 3:1-2. Archelaus ruled Judea, Samaria, and Idumea from 4 BC to AD 6. His maladministration led to his replacement by a procurator or governor. Archelaus is mentioned in Matthew 2:19-23.

Pontius Pilate

After the dismissal of Archelaus in AD 6, a Roman procurator or governor ruled from Caesarea over Judea, Samaria, and Idumea. Pontius Pilate was governor between AD 26 and 36. He proved to be inflexible and self-willed. On three occasions he angered the Jews by his contempt for their religion. First, he had his soldiers enter Jerusalem by night with standards bearing the image of the emperor. Pilate was forced to remove the standards from the city. Second, he set up golden Roman shields in the palace of Herod on Mount Zion. Again, the Jews succeeded in having these offensive objects taken out of Jerusalem. Third, he diverted part of the temple offerings to pay for an aqueduct which increased Jerusalem's water supply. The accompanying violence may be referred to in Luke 13:1.

As the Creed says, Jesus 'suffered under Pontius Pilate, was crucified, dead and buried. The third day he rose from the dead.' Jesus was tried before the Jewish Council on a charge of blasphemy (Matthew 26:57-68; Mark 14:53-64; Luke 22:66-71). But blasphemy was not a capital offence and the Jewish leaders did not have the power to inflict the death penalty. So, Jesus was then tried before Pilate, the Roman governor, on a charge of treason (Matthew 27:11-26; Mark 15:1-15; Luke 23:1-5, 13-25; John 18:28-19:16). Although Pilate could see that Jesus was innocent he allowed him to be crucified so as to avoid a riot. Roman soldiers guarded the tomb of Jesus but were bribed to say that it became empty due to body snatchers (Matthew 27:62-66; 28:11-15). Meanwhile followers of Jesus spread the message of his resurrection (1 Corinthians 15:3-7).

The Zealots

The party of the Zealots probably originated in AD 6 under Judas of Galilee who led a revolt against the imposition of taxes by the pagan emperor. The Zealots were not only hostile to the Romans, they were also antagonistic to the Jewish establishment (the priests and the landowners) who tolerated the occupation. They may well have seen themselves in the tradition of the Maccabees who took up arms against Antiochus Epiphanes.

The First Jewish Revolt

In AD 66, a Zealot led revolt began with a Jewish victory over the Roman governor of Syria. Nero sent his general Vespasian to quell the rebellion. But the revolt had spread like wild fire. It took Vespasian a couple of years to subdue Perea, Samaria, and Idumea. He was ready to attack Jerusalem when news of Nero's death reached him in AD 68. Vespasian was proclaimed emperor by the troops at Caesarea. It was not until AD 69 that he began to lay siege to Jerusalem. He left the task of capturing the city to his son Titus and went to Rome to take charge of the empire. The siege of Jerusalem lasted from April to September in AD 70. The fall of Jerusalem is referred to in the first three gospels (Matthew 24:15-28; Mark 13:14-23; Luke 21:20-24). Between AD 70 and 73 the fortresses of Herodium, Machaerus, and Masada fell to the Romans at great cost to the Jews.

Emperors of Rome

Augustus	31 BC-AD 14
Tiberius	AD 14-37
Caligula	AD 37-41
Claudius	AD 41-54
Nero	AD 54-68
Galba, Otho, Vitellius	AD 68-69
Vespasian	AD 69-79
Titus	AD 79-81
Domitian	AD 81-96
Nerva	AD 96-98
Trajan	AD 98-117
Hadrian	AD 117-138

The Rebuilding of Judaism

After the first Jewish revolt Judaism was rebuilt by the efforts of a leading Jewish teacher and his school at Jamnia in western Judea. Johanan ben Zakkai established a policy of peaceful co-existence with the Romans. His institution classified and codified the traditions surrounding the Jewish law. It educated the teachers of the Jewish law who staffed the synagogues and who comprised a new Jewish Council. There was a parting of the ways between Jews and Christians. The Romans came to see that Christians were not just a Jewish sect. In fact, Christians were excluded from the synagogues by the insertion of a test clause into the daily public prayers around AD 90.

The Second Jewish Revolt

The temple area was deserted and unused until Hadrian decreed in AD 130 that a new city was to be built on the site of Jerusalem. It was to have a temple dedicated to Jupiter and a shrine for the worship of the emperor. Two years later Hadrian issued an edict which forbade the practice of circumcision. A leading Jewish teacher, Akiba, identified a Jew named Simon as the Messiah. Simon became the leader of the second Jewish revolt. Simon was nicknamed Bar Kochba, meaning 'son of the star,' by Akiba. Thereby he was equated with the messianic figure of Numbers 24:17, *I see him, but not now; I behold him, but not near—a star shall come out of Jacob, and a sceptre shall rise out of Israel; it shall crush the borderlands of Moab, and the territory of all the Shethites.*

The revolt lasted from AD 132 to 135. Jerusalem was retaken from the rebels by the Romans. It became a Roman colony. Jews and Jewish Christians were excluded entirely. Only a Gentile Christian community remained. Christians and Jews separated completely. Both were the poorer for it. Christians forgot that Jews were the promise of which they were the fulfilment. Jews did not learn that Christians were the fulfilment of which they were the promise.

Christianity in the Roman World

The early Christians faced opposition from competing faiths, alternative philosophies, and a hostile state. Yet the Christian communities expanded from 1 million (0.6% of population) in the year 100 to 43 million (22.4% of world population) in the year 500.

Competing faiths included the worship of the old Greek and Roman gods, and the worship of the new divine powers and mysterious forces of destiny. The former was a traditional religion which was maintained by the Roman state. Greek gods became Roman gods: Zeus/Jupiter, Hera/Juno, Aphrodite/Venus, Hermes/Mercury, Poseidon/Neptune. The latter began with local deities (Osiris and Isis from Egypt, Adonis from Syria, Attis and Cybele from Phrygia, Mithras from Persia) and ended with widespread mystery religions and secret societies.

Alternative philosophies were taught by the Epicureans, the Cynics, the Stoics, the Pythagoreans, the Platonists, and the Gnostics. These labels refer to schools of thought of many and varied kinds. Epicureans saw the purpose of living realised in this life only. Cynics did not see any purpose or pleasure in this life. Stoics accepted the ups and downs of this life fatalistically. Pythagoreans combined traditional religion and conventional morality. Platonists viewed life at two levels: the heavenly ideal and the earthly real. Gnostics divorced their spiritual life from their earthly life.

A hostile state was evident in the second half of the first century. At this time it became increasingly clear that Christianity was not just a Jewish sect. It was a new religion. It was seen to endanger the security of the Roman state because, at the end of the first century, it refused to pay divine homage to the emperor.

In the first two centuries persecution was local and isolated, personal and informal. Yet, at times, it was intense. In the third century, persecution became universal and connected, public and formal. But, by then, the Christian movement had developed to such an extent that not even the full scale assaults of the Roman empire could destroy it.

In the fourth and fifth centuries, Christians came to express their doctrine of God explicitly. They said that God is the Three in One and the One in Three. He is the Father who creates and sustains. He is the Son who reveals and saves. He is the Spirit who helps and guides. In this Trinitarian fashion, the followers of Jesus were saying that they had experienced *the grace of the Lord Jesus Christ, the love of God, and the fellowship of the Holy Spirit.*

Prayer

Lord God, we have come to know you through the Jewish people who looked forward to the Messiah, the Greeks in whose language the New Testament was transmitted, the Roman authorities who made roads and kept peace for the spread of the Good News. Father God, you create and sustain. Jesus Son of God, you reveal and save. Holy Spirit of God, you help and guide. Thanks and praise be yours as we seek to be your faithful, hopeful, and loving servants. Amen.

Jerusalem

The World of the NT: Select Bibliography

(1) A Valuable Overview of the History of the NT Times
Bruce, F.F., *NT History: The Jews, The Romans, And The Church*

(2) A Brief Summary of the Aspects of NT Background
Brown, R.E., *An Introduction to the NT*, 55-96

(3) The Best of Early 21st Century NT Scholarship in *NIDB*
Bond, H.K., 'Herod, Family, *NIDB*, 2:801-812
Carter, W., 'Roman Empire,' *NIDB*, 4:828-835
Crabbe, L.L., 'Hasmoneans,' *NIDB*, 2:740-748
Crabbe, L.L., 'Maccabees, Maccabean Revolt,' *NIDB*, 3:750-755
Crabbe, L.L., 'Ptolemy,' *NIDB*, 4:685-687
Fine, S. & J.D. Brolley, 'Synagogue,' *NIDB*, 5:416-427
Greenspoon, L., 'Septuagint,' *NIDB*, 5:170-177
Heard, W., 'Zealot,' *NIDB*, 5:958-961
Parsenios, G.L., 'Greek Religion and Philosophy,' *NIDB*, 2:681-698
Perkins, P., 'Gnosticism,' *NIDB*, 2:581-584
Regev, E., 'Sadducees,' *NIDB*, 5:32-36
Schnabel, E.J., 'Pharisees, *NIDB*, 4:485-496
Schowalter, D.M., 'Roman Religions,' *NIDB*, 4:836-841
Vanderkam, J.C., 'Essenes,' *NIDB*, 2:315-316
Vanderkam, J.C., 'Judaism,' *NIDB*, 3:424-435

(4) An Excellent Summary of the Major Issues in NT Background
Wright, N.T. & M.F. Bird, *The NT in Its World*, 86-169

2 The Letter to the Hebrews
The pioneer and perfecter of our faith

Overview of Hebrews
(adapted from Raymond Brown)

Date: 60s or 80s.
From: Not specified.
To: Not identified but probably to followers of Jesus attracted to Judaism in Rome.
Origin: Unknown author.
Outline: 1:1-3 Introduction
        1:4-4:13 Superiority of Jesus as God's Son
        4:14-7:28 Superiority of Jesus' priesthood
        8:1-10:18 Superiority of Jesus' sacrifice
        10:19-12:29 Faith and endurance
        13:1-19 Injunctions about practice
        13:20-25 Conclusion

Message

It has been noted that Hebrews begins like a treatise (1:1-4), continues like a sermon (1:5-13:19), and concludes like a letter (13:20-25). The content of the book can be outlined in a number of ways.

First, Albert Vanhoye (followed by Hugh Montefiore) very cleverly detected a chiastic structure between the introduction (1:1-4) and the conclusion (13:20-25) as follows:

I   Eschatology: Jesus is better than the angels (1:5-2:18)
II   Ecclesiology: Jesus is the faithful and merciful great high priest (3:1-5:10)
III   Sacrifice: Jesus, the priest after the order of Melchizedek, offered himself once for all (5:11-10:39)
IV   Ecclesiology: Jesus is the pioneer and perfecter of faith (11:1-12:13)
V   Eschatology: Jesus is the same yesterday and today and for ever (12:14-13:19)

The theme of I matches the theme of V (Eschatology) and the theme of II matches the theme of IV (Ecclesiology). The central theme of III (Sacrifice) develops the intriguing explanation of Jesus as a priest for ever according to the order of Melchizedek (Psalm 110:4).

Second, F.F. Bruce noted five warnings in the midst of teaching about the person and work of Christ:

1   On the one hand, the book says that Jesus is God's final revelation and is better than the angels (1:1-14). On the other hand, it says that the readers must beware of drifting away – drifting from their course (2:1-4).

2   On the one hand, the book states that Jesus is the pioneer of salvation and is better than Moses (2:5-3:6). On the other hand, it states that the readers must be beware of hardening their hearts - growing stubborn (3:7-4:13).

3   On the one hand, the book observes that Jesus is the great high priest, implying that he is better than the earthly high priest in the Jerusalem temple (4:14-5:10). On the other hand, it

observes the danger of falling away so that the readers must beware of becoming sluggish - being lax or lazy (5:11-6:20).
4   On the one hand, the book speaks about Jesus as the priestly king of a new order and the mediator of a better covenant (7:1-10:25). On the other hand, it speaks about the readers who must beware of shrinking back and being lost (10:26-39).
5   On the one hand, the book teaches that Jesus is the pioneer and perfecter of faith and is the embodiment of something better (11:1-12:11). On the other hand, it teaches that the readers must beware of refusing to hear the message of God (12:12-29).
As Floyd Filson has shown, the book concludes in 13:1-25 with a fourfold pattern: (1) varied teaching, (2) formal benediction, (3) personal greetings, and (4) closing short benediction.

Third, Raymond Brown indicated a sequence of themes between the introduction and the conclusion:
1   Superiority of Jesus as God's Son:
    Over angels (1:4-2:18)
    Over Moses (3:1-4:13)
2   Superiority of Jesus' priesthood:
    Over Levitical priesthood (4:14-7:28)
3   Superiority of Jesus' sacrifice:
    Over the old covenant (8:1-13)
    Over the earthly sanctuary (9:1-10:18)
4   Superiority of Jesus' priestly work:
    Leading to perseverance (10:19-39)
    Leading to loyalty (11:1-40)
    Leading to discipline (12:1-13)
    Leading to reverence (12:14-29)
5   Final exhortation (13:1-19)

Milieu and Meaning

Were the readers suffering persecution?

Hebrews 10:32-34 recalls earlier times: *But recall those earlier days when, after you had been enlightened, you endured a hard struggle with sufferings, sometimes being publicly exposed to abuse and persecution, and sometimes being partners with those so treated. For you had compassion for those who were in prison, and you cheerfully accepted the plundering of your possessions, knowing that you yourselves possessed something better and more lasting.* Hebrews 12:4 looks to the future: *In your struggle against sin you have not yet resisted to the point of shedding your blood.*

Was the temple still standing?

Hebrews 9:6-9 compares the temple with the tabernacle in Old Testament times: *Such preparations having been made, the priests go continually into the first tent to carry out their ritual duties; but only the high priest goes into the second, and he but once a year, and not without taking the blood that he offers for himself and for the sins committed unintentionally by the people. By this the Holy Spirit indicates that the way into the sanctuary has not yet been disclosed as long as the first tent is still standing. This is a symbol of the present time, during which gifts and sacrifices are offered that cannot perfect the conscience of the worshipper.* Hebrews 10:1-2 contrasts the shadow and the true form: *Since the law has only a shadow of the good things to come and not the true form of these realities, it can never, by the same sacrifices that are continually offered year after year, make perfect those who approach. Otherwise, would they not have ceased being offered, since the worshippers, cleansed once for all, would no longer have any consciousness of sin?*

Why does the writer mention the mysterious Melchizedek?

Hebrews 7:1-28 speaks of the priestly order of Melchizedek and gives an exposition of Psalm 110:4 in this way:

7:1-3 ***of Melchizedek***
Without father, without mother, without genealogy, having neither beginning of days nor end of life, but resembling the Son of God

7:4-10 ***a priest***
... he remains a priest for ever. See how great he is!

7:11-12 ***according to the order***
another priest arising according to the order of Melchizedek, rather than one according to the order of Aaron

7:13-14 ***you are***
it is evident that our Lord was descended from Judah

7:15-28 ***for ever***
a Son who has been made perfect for ever

As F.F. Bruce says, 'it is not the type which determines the antitype, but the antitype which determines the type; Jesus is not portrayed after the pattern of Melchizedek, but Melchizedek is "made conformable to the Son of God."'

The book is almost a collection of sermons with the ending of a letter. It has been dated in the 60s or in the 80s of the first century. My preference is for the years before the fall of Jerusalem in AD 70. We do not know who it is from but we have a fair idea of who it is written to. It appears to be written to Christians who are attracted to Jewish ways and who live around Jerusalem or Rome. Although the authorship, location and date of the book are unknown, it is a wonderful balance of teaching and living. Throughout its intricate argument, it confronts the possible heresy of leaving the truth of Jesus for the error of not appreciating all that Jesus has done.

According to Howard Marshall there are five significant elements of the book of Hebrews:

First, Jesus is understood as the Son of God, superior to all other figures, including Moses, as the mediator of the new covenant.

Second, the concept of priesthood is central. Jesus Christ is the high priest, qualified for the role due to two things: his identity as the Son of God and his incarnation and human experience.

Third, Jesus sacrificed himself in his death and entered into the heavenly Temple to make a once-for-all offering for sin. Unusually the resurrection of Jesus has little significance in the theology of the book.

Fourth, forgiveness is impossible other than by the offering of Christ and forgiveness is impossible for those who turn away from Christ.

Fifth, the Christian life is understood as a pilgrimage or journey in faith.

Mission

The Letter to the Hebrews tells us to go in and on and out (4:14-16; 6:1-3; 12:1-3; 13:12-14). As Frederick Buechner says, 'Faith is better understood as a verb than as a noun, as a process than as a possession.' Yes, in the letter to the Hebrews, faith is going.

First, faith is going in. *Let us therefore approach the throne of grace with boldness, so that we may receive mercy and find grace to help in time of need. (Hebrews 4:16)* We go in to God's throne with boldness. At God's throne is Jesus our high priest. He sits exalted at the Father's right hand. In the Old Testament Tabernacle, there was the mercy seat, the cover of the Ark, where the earthly high priest went on the Day of Atonement and offered a sacrifice for sins (Exodus 25:17). In the heavenly sanctuary, there is the mercy seat where the heavenly high priest went once and for all and offered himself for our sins. As Tom Long notes, 'What does the church see when it looks into the face of its great high priest? . . . It sees a God who stoops down from the holy heights to bear our griefs and carry our sorrows.' No wonder that we can go in with boldness to receive mercy and find grace to help, mercy for past sins and grace for future help.

Second, faith is going on. *Therefore let us go on toward perfection. (Hebrews 6:1)* We go on from basic beliefs and practices to perfection or maturity. It looks as if existing Jewish beliefs and practices were being used as a foundation on which the readers were building their understanding of Christian truth: repentance, faith, baptism, laying on of hands, resurrection, and judgement. Such a foundation is adequate for a while but it remains a foundation. The original readers must press on to deeper appreciation of the person and work of Christ. Like them, we have a foundation on which we are building our understanding of Christian truth: conversion and baptism, community and communion, and so on. Our foundation is adequate for a while but it is still a foundation on which we must build by God's grace.

The comment about receiving a completeness in Christ reminds us of a terrible warning: *For it is impossible to restore again to repentance those who have once been enlightened, and have tasted the heavenly gift, and have shared in the Holy Spirit, and have tasted the goodness of the word of God and the powers of the age to come, and then have fallen away, since on their own they are crucifying again the Son of God and are holding him up to contempt. (Hebrews 6:4-6)* In the words of F.F. Bruce, 'People are frequently immunized against a disease by being inoculated with a mild form of it, or with a related but milder disease. And in the spiritual realm experience suggests that it is possible to be "immunized" against Christianity by being inoculated with something which, for the time being, looks so like the real thing that it is generally mistaken for it.'

Third, faith is going out. *Let us then go to him outside the camp and bear the abuse he endured. (Hebrews 13:13)* We go out to the world which needs our life-transforming belief and practice. The original readers were tempted to revert to Jewish understandings of God, to the Old Testament promises of God: angels (Hebrews 1-2), Moses (Hebrews 3), Joshua (Hebrews 4), the high priest (Hebrews 5), the Day of Atonement sacrifices (Hebrews 9-10). But for the original readers the future lay not with the camp of Judaism but with the Gentile mission, with the New Testament fulfilment of God's purposes. In the words of Tom Long, 'If Jesus went outside and suffered public abuse in order to make *his* sacrifice, then his brothers and sisters should be willing to follow him to make ours.' We are tempted to revert to traditional understandings of God's people, to confuse the means with the end, to identify the church with a building. A building is important as a means to an end. We meet here, to minister there. The church is the people who go in to Christ, go on with Christ, and go out for Christ. If faith is going in and on and out, faith is waiting. Faith is *looking to Jesus the pioneer and perfecter of our faith (Hebrews 12:2)*.

We have thought about faith: going in and on and out. In Søren Kierkegaard's parable of the geese every week the geese would gather inside the barnyard and be uplifted, inspired, and moved by the philosopher goose's message. But what did they do? What will you and I do? Are we ready to fly? Or will we just talk? In another era they used to say that there were too many people who were content to sing 'Standing on the promises' while they were just sitting on the premises! Let's get out of the barnyard and into the world for Christ our Lord! Let us go in and on and out!

The Letter to the Hebrews also says, *Jesus Christ is the same yesterday and today and for ever* (Hebrews 13:8).

The same yesterday?

Yesterday was the time when Jesus Christ, God's only Son, our Lord, suffered under Pontius Pilate, was crucified, died and was buried, and descended into the realm of death. Yesterday was the time when, according to Hebrews 5:7, *In the days of his flesh, Jesus offered up prayers and supplications, with loud cries and tears, to the one who was able to save him from death, and he was heard because of his reverent submission.* Some people have interpreted this as the prayer of Jesus in Gethsemane, *My Father, if it is possible, let this cup pass from me; yet not what I want but what you want.(Matthew 26:39)* Other people think that it refers to Jesus' cry of despair from the cross, *My God, my God, why have you forsaken me? (Matthew 27:46; Psalm 22:1)*

Jesus, the Jew of Nazareth, is an example of reverent submission by his prayers of tears, tears for a needy world and tears to a gracious Father. Accordingly, Hebrews 5:9 says that *he learned obedience through what he suffered* and that *he became the source of eternal salvation.* As Tom Long comments, 'Not only is he compassionate toward those who have lost sight of the truth that they are God's very own children, Jesus can also take them by the hand and lead them home.'

Yes, we rejoice that the people of God have always told the story of yesterday in their experience of Jesus Christ. We thank God that Jesus *learned obedience through what he suffered* and that *he became the source of eternal salvation.*

The same today?

Today is the time when Jesus Christ, having risen from the dead on the third day, and having ascended into heaven, is seated at the right hand of God, the almighty Father. Today is the time when, according to Hebrews 4:14-16, *Since, then, we have a great high priest who has passed though the heavens, Jesus, the Son of God, let us hold fast to our confession. For we do not have a high priest who is unable to sympathise with our weaknesses, but we have one who in every respect has been tested as we are, yet without sin. Let us therefore approach the throne of grace with boldness, so that we may receive mercy and find grace to help in time of need.*

Of course, a priest is the distinctive picture of Jesus in the Letter to the Hebrews. On the one hand, a priest goes to people on behalf of God. On the other hand, a priest goes to God on behalf of people. And Jesus is more than a priest, he is the great high priest. No wonder that we have confidence and hope to bring our prayers to God through him. The great preacher Fred Craddock has put it well: 'He was as we are, and therefore he will help; he was not as we are, and therefore he can.'

The church has always told the story of today in its experience of Jesus Christ. We are thankful that *we have a great high priest . . . Jesus, the Son of God.* Therefore, today, we can *receive mercy and find grace to help in time of need.*

The same for ever?

For ever is the time when Jesus Christ will come from God's right hand to judge the living and the dead. *For ever* is the time when, according to Hebrews 7:25, *Consequently he is able for all time to save those who approach God through him, since he always lives to make intercession for them.*

The author of Hebrews carries his argument further in chapter 9:27-28, *And just as it is appointed for mortals to die once, and after that the judgement, so Christ, having been offered once to bear the sins of many, will appear a second time, not to deal with sin, but to save those who are eagerly waiting for him.*

The people of God have always told the story of for ever in its experience of Jesus Christ.

The same yesterday, today, for ever?

To sum up. Hebrews 13:8 tells us that *Jesus Christ is the same yesterday and today and for ever.* Jesus established a personal relationship by suffering for his followers yesterday. Jesus maintains a personal relationship with his followers today. Jesus will sustain such a personal relationship for ever.

In the previous verse, Hebrews 13:7, the author urges his readers to remember their leaders. These leaders had spoken the word of God to them. These leaders had practised what they preached. These leaders had set a fine example. The outcome of their way of life is worth considering. Their faith is worth imitating. In other words, these leaders are like their Leader, Jesus Christ. Accordingly, *Since we are surrounded by so great a cloud of witnesses, let us also lay aside every weight and the sin that clings so closely, and let us run with perseverance the race that is set before us, looking to Jesus the pioneer and perfecter of our faith. (Hebrews 12:1-2)*

Prayer

Lord, help us to go in and approach the throne of grace with boldness, so that we may receive mercy and find grace to help in time of need. Lord, help us to go on towards maturity, so that having been enlightened and having shared in the Holy Spirit we may live by faith all our days. Lord, help us to go out, so that we may join Jesus not within a closed introverted community but outside in the worldwide mission of God's people, Jew and Gentile.

Lord, we seek to go in and on and out because Jesus Christ is the same yesterday and today and for ever. Yesterday Jesus learned obedience through what he suffered and became the source of eternal salvation. Today Jesus is the great high priest, the Son of God through whom we receive mercy and find grace to help. For ever is the time when Jesus will come from God's right hand to judge the living and the dead. Lord, hear our prayers through the one who is the same yesterday and today and for ever. Amen.

Hebrews: Select Bibliography

Brown, R.E., *An Introduction to the NT*, 683-704
Bruce, F.F., *The Epistle to the Hebrews*
Bruce, F.F., 'To the Hebrews' or 'To the Essenes'? *NTS*, 9:217-232 (1963)
Buechner, F., 'Faith,' *Beyond Words*, 108-110
Craddock, F.B., 'The Letter to the Hebrews,' *NIB*, 12:1-173
deSilva, D.A., 'Hebrews, Letter to the,' *NIDB*, 2:779-786
deSilva, D.A., *An Introduction to the NT*, 686-719
Dunn, J.D.G., *Jesus according to the NT*, 141-155
Dunn, J.D.G., *Neither Jew nor Greek*, 91-96
Filson, F.V., *'Yesterday'*
Isaacs, M.E., 'Hebrews,' *Mercer Commentary on the Bible*, 1267-1281
Jobes, K.H., *Letters to the Church*, 23-143
Köstenberger, A.J., *Handbook on Hebrews through Revelation*, 1-65
Kümmel, W.G., *Introduction to the NT*, 388-403
Long, T.G., *Hebrews: Interpretation*
Marshall, I.H., *NT Theology Many Witnesses One Gospel*, 605-627
Montefiore, H.W., *The Epistle to the Hebrews*
Powell, M.A., *Introducing the NT*, 443-459
Puskas, C.B., *Hebrews, the General Letters, and Revelation*, 10-39
Rowston, D., *A Bird's Eye View of the Bible*, 214-217
Wright, N.T. & M.F. Bird, *The NT in Its World*, 710-729

3 The Letter of James
Our glorious Lord Jesus Christ

Overview of James
(adapted from Raymond Brown)

Date: If pseudonymous, in the 80s or 90s. [If genuine, before the death of James in AD 62.]
To: The 12 tribes in the Dispersion, followers of Jesus who appreciate Judaism outside Palestine.
Origin: The Lord's brother James before his death, or a disciple who admires James' image.
Outline:
- 1:1   Greetings
- 1:2-18   Trials and temptations
- 1:19-27   Words and deeds
- 2:1-9   Partiality toward the rich
- 2:10-13   The whole law
- 2:14-26   Faith and works
- 3:1-12   The tongue's power
- 3:13-18   Wisdom from above
- 4:1-10   Desires and division
- 4:11-12   Judging another and judging the law
- 4:13-17   Boasting and arrogance
- 5:1-6   Warning to the rich
- 5:7-11   Patience
- 5:12-20   Admonitions

Message

The content of the Letter of James defies simplification. Apart from the beginning (1:1), it is not a letter. The book is like Jewish wisdom literature, it employs the Greek rhetorical device of diatribe, and it has connections with sayings of Jesus.

First, according to Martin Dibelius, it is a collection of admonitions linked by catchwords:
> Rejoice in testings (1:2-18)
> Hear and do the word (1:19-27)
> Beware of favouritism toward rich and against poor (2:1-12)
> Show mercy (2:13)
> Show faith in works of mercy (2:14-26)
> Tame the tongue (3:1-12)
> Seek heavenly wisdom (3:13-18)
> Be humble (4:1-10)
> Don't slander (4:11-12)
> Don't boast about tomorrow (4:13-17)
> Let the rich be warned (5:1-6)
> Be patient (5:7-12)
> Be prayerful (5:13-18)
> Rescue the sinful (5:19-20)

Catchwords are found in 1:4-5 (*lacking ... lacking*), 12-13 (*temptation ... tempted ... tempted ... tempts*), 15-18 (*gives birth ... gave birth*), 26-27 (*religious ... religion ... religion*); 2:12-13 (*judged ... judgement ... judgement*); 3:11-14 (*brackish/bitter ... bitter*), 17-18 (*peaceable ... peace ... peace*): 5:9, 12 (*judged ... Judge ... condemnation/judgement*), 16-20 (*sins ... sinner*).

Second, the Letter has been analysed by Ralph Martin in terms of three themes:
    Address and three themes (1:1-27)
    Rich and poor (2:1-26)
        Compare 1:9-11, 22-25
    Tongue (3:1-4:12)
        Compare 1:5-8, 19-21
    Trials (4:13-5:6)
        Compare 1:2-4, 12-18
    Three themes and conclusion (5:7-20)

Third, the topics of the Letter have been brought together under the heading of the obedience of faith by Alan Culpepper:

I	Introduction (1:1)
II	The obedience of faith (1:2-27)
III	The obedience of faith in worship and works (2:1-26)
IV	The obedience of faith in words and wisdom (3:1-18)
V	The obedience of faith in community (4:1-5:6)
VI	The obedience of faith in patience, oaths, and prayer (5:7-18)
VII	Conclusion (5:19-20)

Milieu and Meaning

The book is a collection of sermon outlines in the shape of a letter. It is an ethical scrapbook or a moral notebook whose theme is Christian godliness or practical Christianity. Traditionally, the book has been identified with the brother of the Lord, James, who died as a martyr in AD 62. If so, the book could have been written in the 40s or 50s. On the other hand, for reasons of its Greek style, its view of the law and its slow recognition, the book has been understood to be written by an admirer of James during the 80s or 90s. In other words, the authorship, location and date of the book are uncertain. However, it remains as a deposit of wise words to be lived out in wise deeds.

As we look at the book of James, we find that it instructs Christians ancient and modern in the art of living. In so doing, the book stresses four things. First, favouritism is evil. We are not to love our well dressed 'neighbour' and hate our poorly dressed 'enemy' (2:1-4). Second, faith and action are both essential. We are not to major on belief and minor on practice (2:14-17). Third, loose talk is perilous. We are not to forget that we shall be judged by our own words (3:7-10). Fourth, the wealthy are warned. Great riches bring great privileges and great responsibilities (5:1-6). The book of James in giving advice to the Christian is saying in effect: 'Good deeds do not make a good Christian but a good Christian does good deeds'.

According to Howard Marshall, there are five significant elements of the book of James:

First, human beings are answerable to God's judgement through Christ, who is near.

Second, God's word and wisdom are provided to enable believers to develop maturity.

Third, faith needs to be expressed in action.

Fourth, life lived according to God's law involves loving one's neighbour and forbids partiality.

Fifth, life is to be lived in dependence on God through prayer.

Mission

The Wikipedia article traces the origin of phrase **'What would Jesus do?'** to the concept of *The Imitation of Christ,* a book written by Thomas à Kempis in the 15th century. In 1896 Charles Sheldon wrote a novel *In His Steps: What Would Jesus Do?* Apparently the novel inspired Walter Rauschenbusch who promulgated the Social Gospel starting in 'Hell's Kitchen' New York City from 1885. In the 1990s bracelets with the letters WWJD became popular.

So the four letters WWJD have become a popular way of asking 'What would Jesus do?' Indeed, the letter of James seems to be answering the same question. James Dunn, gives seven examples of James utilising the Jesus tradition.

First, James answers the question, Does anyone lack wisdom? (James 1:5) by referring back to Jesus, *Ask and you will receive ... (Matthew 7:7)*

Second, James answers the question, Has God chosen the poor to be heirs of the kingdom? (James 2:5) by referring back to Jesus' promise, *Blessed are the poor in spirit, for theirs is the kingdom of heaven.(Matthew 5:3)*

Third, James answers the question, What is the relation between laughter and mourning? (James 4:9) by referring to Jesus' great reversal, *Blessed are those who mourn, for they will be comforted.(Matthew 5:4)*

Fourth, James answers the question, What is the relation between humility and exaltation? (James 4:10) by referring to Jesus' words, *All who exalt themselves will be humbled, and all who humble themselves will be exalted. (Matthew 23:12)*

Fifth, James answers the question, What is the fate of the rich? (James 5:1) by referring to Jesus' warning, *But woe to you who are rich, for you have received your consolation ... (Luke 6:24-25)*

Sixth, James answers the question, What happens to riches? (James 5:2-3a) by referring to Jesus' alternative exhortation, *Store up for yourself treasures in heaven. (Matthew 6:20)*

Seventh, James answers the question, Should one swear or use an oath? (James 5:12) by referring to Jesus' great simplicity, *Do not swear at all ... Let your word be 'Yes, Yes' or 'No. No' ... (Matthew 5:34-37)*

As James Dunn says, 'In the letter of James we see teaching of Jesus which has been absorbed and become the lifeblood of a teacher's teaching and a community's paraenesis.' (Paraenesis transliterates a Greek word meaning instruction.)

Prayer

Lord, help us to answer the question, 'What would Jesus do?'
As we think of the teaching of Jesus and James, we pray for
practical gifts:
> wisdom not foolishness,
> impartiality not favouritism,
> empathy not insensitivity,
> humility not pride,
> generosity not selfishness,
> service of God not service of wealth,
> simple speech not filthy language.

So we ask for your grace and peace to live out the wise words
in wise deeds. Amen.

James: Select Bibliography

Bauckham, R., 'James,' *Eerdmans Commentary on the Bible*, 1483-1492
Brown, R.E., *An Introduction to the NT*, 725-747
Culpepper, R.A., 'James,' *Mercer Commentary on the Bible*, 1283-1294
deSilva, D.A., *An Introduction to the NT*, 720-743
Dunn, J.D.G., *Beginning from Jerusalem*, 1122-1147
Dunn, J.D.G., *Jesus according to the NT*, 158-162
Jobes, K.H., *Letters to the Church*, 147-232
Johnson, L.T., 'The Letter of James,' *NIB*, 12:175-225
Köstenberger, A.J., *Handbook on Hebrews through Revelation*, 67-97
Kümmel, W.G., *Introduction to the NT*, 403-416
Marshall, I.H., *NT Theology Many Witnesses One Gospel*, 628-641
Martin, R.P., *James*
Painter, J., 'James, Letter of,' *NIDB*, 3:189-194
Powell, M.A., *Introducing the NT*, 461-477
Puskas, C.B., *Hebrews, the General Letters, and Revelation*, 40-66
Rowston, D., *A Bird's Eye View of the Bible*, 205-207
Wright, N.T. & M.F. Bird, *The NT in Its World*, 730-736, 740-749, 754

4 The First Letter of Peter
The shepherd and guardian of our souls

Overview of 1 Peter
(adapted from Raymond Brown)

Date: If written by Peter, 60-63; if written by a disciple of Peter, between 70 and 90.
To: Followers of Jesus in northern Asia Minor.
Origin: By Peter, using a secretary; or by a disciple of Peter, carrying on his heritage in Rome.
Unity: Majority of scholars opt for unity; but minority see two documents joined: one in which persecution was possible (1:3-4:11) and the other in which persecution is actual (4:12-5:11).
Outline: 1:1-2   Opening formula
           1:3-2:10   Christian identity
           2:11-3:12 Good witness in pagan world
           3:13-5:11 Christian behaviour in face of hostility
           5:12-14   Concluding formula

Message

There are three approaches to the content of the First Letter of Peter.

First, E.G. Selwyn distinguished doctrinal sections from hortatory sections between the opening and closing of the letter:

I	Introduction (1:1-2)
II	First doctrinal section: The living hope (1:3-12)
III	First hortatory section: Be holy (1:13-2:3)
IV	Second doctrinal section: God's own people (2:4-10)
V	Second hortatory section: Accept the authority of every human institution (2:11-3:12)
VI	Third doctrinal section: Christ's suffering (3:13-4:19)
VII	Third hortatory section: Tend the flock of God (5:1-11)
VIII	Conclusion (5:12-14)

Thereby the letter balanced the indicative of the Good News with its imperative.

Second, in the search for an explanation of the First Letter of Peter, scholars have identified echoes of baptismal prayers in 1:18-20 and 3:18-19 and citations of the Old Testament in 1:24-25; 2:6-8, 10, 21-25; 3:10-12; 4:18; and 5:5. Accordingly, there are a couple of suggestions. The first part of the letter (1:3 to 4:11) seems to consider persecution to be only a possibility for some readers, whereas the second part of the letter (4:12 to 5:11) appears to admit persecution to be an actuality for other readers. Some scholars (e.g. C.F.D. Moule) suggest that the letter takes a baptismal sermon in 1:3 to 4:11 and applies it to a new situation of persecution in 4:12-5:11. As a result, a second approach is as follows:

I	Introduction (1:1-2)
II	In view of possible persecution (1:3-4:11)
	Remember the living hope and be holy.
	Remember that you are God's people and be good citizens.
	Remember Christ's suffering and be good stewards of grace.
III	In view of actual persecution (4:12-5:11)

       Remember that you are sharing Christ's suffering and glorify his name.
       Remember that I am an elder and follow my example in leadership and humility.
IV   Conclusion (5:12-14)

Third, a topical outline is given by David Bartlett:

I   Greetings (1:1-2)
II   Praise to God (1:3-12)
III   God's holy people (1:13-2:10)
IV   Life in exile (2:11-4:11)
V   Steadfast in faith (4:12-5:11)
VI   Final greetings (5:12-14)

Milieu and Meaning

Although some scholars believe that it is written by a disciple of Peter between AD 70 and 90, I think that the letter is written by Peter with the secretarial support of Silvanus before the Great Fire of Rome in AD 64. It is directed towards believers in the northern area of Asia Minor. Tacitus, the Roman historian, says that Nero shifted the blame for the Great Fire from himself to the Christians and had them convicted 'not only of arson but also for hatred of humanity.' Eusebius, the Christian historian, writes that Nero 'went so far as to cause the slaughter of the apostles ... Paul was beheaded in Rome itself and ... Peter likewise was crucified.'

Howard Marshall notes five significant themes in First Peter:

First, the letter's theology is expressed in strong dependence on

41

the Old Testament and in evident awareness of believers as the people of God.

Second, the hopeful aspect of faith is emphasised as belief in God who raises the dead and guards his people.

Third, Jesus Christ is understood in terms of stone and servant imagery.

Fourth, the reference to Christ's preaching to the spirits in prison is unique in the NT.

Fifth, persecution is recognised as an opportunity for witness and there is a positive attitude towards living as Christians in the world despite the world's sin and opposition.

Mission

Of particular relevance in today's church and world are First Peter's treatment of baptism and response to persecution.

Baptism:

Dale Moody has helpfully analysed six meanings of baptism in the New Testament; three are major and three are minor.

First, purification means that we are cleansed and forgiven by God. Second, identification means that we belong to God. Third, incorporation means that we join God's people.

Fourth, rebirth indicates that we begin to grow to maturity. There may be hints of this meaning in 1 Peter 1:3, 23, *By his great mercy he has given us a new birth into a living hope ... You have been born anew ... through the living and enduring word of God.* Fifth, salvation indicates that experience God's help. As 1 Peter 3:21 says, *And baptism ... now saves you ... as an appeal to God for a good conscience, through the resurrection of Jesus Christ.* Sixth, illumination indicates that we find God's guidance. (See Hebrews 6:4, *For it is impossible to restore again to repentance those who have once been enlightened ...*)

The text of Nestle-Aland, *Novum Testamentum Graece* indicates that there may well be traces of baptismal liturgy in First Peter:

You know that you were ransomed not with perishable things like silver or gold
from the futile ways inherited from your ancestors
but with the precious blood of Christ, like that of a lamb without defect or blemish
He was destined before the foundation of the world
but was revealed at the end of the ages
for your sake through him you have come to trust in God
who raised him from the dead and gave him glory
so that your faith and hope are set on God (1:18-21)

For Christ also suffered for sins once for all
the righteous for the unrighteous
in order to bring you to God
He was put to death in the flesh
but made alive in the spirit
in which also to the spirits in prison
he went and made a proclamation (3:18-19)

Today's church can learn from 1 Peter and other New Testament writings in the matter of baptism. Do we practise the rite of Christian initiation in terms of the New Testament? Does our practice convey the full meaning of Christian baptism? Do we relate the act of baptism in our churches to the themes of purification, identification, incorporation, rebirth, salvation, and illumination?

Persecution:

If, as C.F.D. Moule suggests, 1 Peter refers to possible persecution (1:3-4:11) and to actual persecution (4:12-5:11), the letter speaks to church groups in *Pontus, Galatia, Cappadocia, Asia, and Bithynia (1:1)* facing a hostile world.

On the one hand, some of the churches face possible persecution:

In this you rejoice, even if now for a little while you have had to suffer various trials, so that the genuineness of your faith ... may be found to result in praise and glory and honour when Jesus Christ is revealed.(1:6-7)
Conduct yourselves honourably among the Gentiles, so that, though they malign you as evildoers, they may see your honourable deeds and glorify God when he comes to judge. (2:12)
Do not repay evil for evil or abuse for abuse; but, on the contrary, repay with a blessing ... but in your hearts sanctify Christ as Lord. Always be ready to make your defence to anyone who demands from you an account of the hope that is in you.(3:9, 15)

On the other hand, some of the churches face actual persecution:

Beloved, do not be surprised at the fiery ordeal that is taking place among you to test you, as though something strange were happening to you. But rejoice in so far as you are sharing Christ's sufferings, so that you may also be glad and shout for joy when his glory is revealed. (4:12-13)
... you know that your brothers and sisters throughout the world are undergoing the same kinds of suffering. And after you have suffered for a little while, the God of all grace, who has called you to his eternal glory in Christ, will himself restore, support, strengthen, and establish you. (5:9-10)

In either situation the readers are given directions:

But even if you do suffer for doing what is right, you are blessed. Do not fear what they fear, and do not be intimidated, but in your hearts sanctify Christ as Lord. Always be ready to make your defence to anyone who demands from you an account of the hope that is in you. (3:14-15)
Yet if any of you suffers as a Christian, do not consider it a disgrace, but glorify God because you bear this name. For the time has come for judgement to begin with the household of God; if it begins with us, what will be the end for those who do not obey the gospel of God? (4:16-17)

By the second half of the first century, it became increasingly clear to the Roman authorities that Christianity was not just a Jewish sect. It was a new religion and was seen to endanger the security of the Roman state because it refused to pay divine homage to the emperor. Although persecution was local and isolated, and personal and informal, there were times when persecution was intense, especially during the Great Fire under Nero and in the face of edicts that identified Domitian as 'Lord and God.'

By the second half of the third century, persecution became universal and connected, and public and formal. But by then the Christian movement had developed to such an extent that not even the full scale assaults of the Roman Empire could destroy it.

Today's church can also learn from 1 Peter and other New Testament writings in the matter of persecution. Do we appreciate the world's responses to Christian faith in our own lands and in regions beyond? Some Christians suffer sullen indifference or secular hostility. Are such people of faith prepared to suffer for doing right and to be ready with an appropriate word of explanation for their hope? Other Christians suffer at the hands of extremist religious groups or hostile political states. Are these devout followers of Jesus prepared to suffer as Christians and to give glory to the God and Father of the Lord Jesus Christ?

Prayer

Lord, we recognise the fact of suffering as Christians. At times it is through sullen indifference or secular hostility. At other times it is because of extremist religious groups or hostile political states. Help us as followers of Jesus, whether persecution of our faith is possible or actual, always to be ready to make our defence to anyone who demands from us an account of the hope that is in us; always not to consider it an embarrassment but to rejoice in so far as we are sharing Christ's sufferings. We remember that we have been called to God's eternal glory in Christ. We face the future with confidence that God will restore, support, strengthen, and establish us by his grace and peace in Christ. Amen.

1 Peter: Select Bibliography

Achtemeier, P., 'Peter, First Letter of,' *NIDB*, 4:462-468
Bartlett, D.L., 'The First Letter of Peter,' *NIB*, 12:227-319
Brown, R.E., *An Introduction to the NT*, 705-724
deSilva, D.A., *An Introduction to the NT*, 744-766
Dunn, J.D.G., *Beginning from Jerusalem*, 1147-1166
Dunn, J.D.G., *Jesus according to the NT*, 162-167
Dunn, J.D.G., *Neither Jew nor Greek*, 727-729
Jobes, K.H., *Letters to the Church*, 267-352
Kelly, J.N.D., *The Epistles of Peter & of Jude*, 1-221
Köstenberger, A.J., *Handbook on Hebrews through Revelation*, 99-145
Kümmel, W.G., *Introduction to the NT*, 416-425
Marshall, I.H., *NT Theology Many Witnesses One Gospel*, 642-659
Moody, D., *The Word of Truth*, 460-467
Moule, C.F.D., 'The Nature and Purpose of I Peter,' *NTS*, 3:1-11 (1956)
Powell, M.A., *Introducing the NT*, 479-495
Puskas, C.B., *Hebrews, the General Letters, and Revelation*, 67-91
Rowston, D., *A Bird's Eye View of the Bible*, 225-227
Selwyn, E.G., *The First Epistle of St Peter*
Stanton, G.N., '1 Peter,' *Eerdmans Commentary on the Bible*, 1493-1503
Wright, N.T. & M.F. Bird, *The NT in Its World*, 756-763, 770-777, 781-783

5 The Letter of Jude & the Second Letter of Peter
Our only Master and Lord, our Lord and Saviour

Overview of Jude & 2 Peter
(adapted from Raymond Brown)

Jude
Date: Minority of scholars place it in 50s; majority in 90s.
From/To: *From* Palestine where the brothers of Jesus were major figures. *To* followers of Jesus influenced by Palestinian churches.
Origin: If pseudonymous, by one for whom the brothers of Jesus were authoritative teachers. [If genuine, by Jude the Lord's brother.]
Outline:
- 1-2   Opening formula
- 3-4   Occasion: Contend for the faith
- 5-10   Three examples of disobedience
- 11-13   Three more examples
- 14-19   Prophecies of Enoch and of apostles
- 20-23   Appeal for faith
- 24-25   Concluding doxology

2 Peter
Date: After Pauline letters, 1 Peter & Jude; in 2nd cent. AD.
To/From: *To* followers of Jesus in Asia Minor who knew Paul's letters and 1 Peter. *From* Rome.
Origin: Pseudonymous, by one who wished to present a final message from Peter.
Outline:
- 1:1-2   Opening formula
- 1:3-21   Exhortation to progress in virtue
- 2:1-22   Condemnation of false teachers
- 3:1-16   Delay of the second coming
- 3:17-18   Concluding exhortation and doxology

Message

The Letter of Jude is a 'letter of exhortation' according to N.T. Wright and M.F. Bird. It deals with heretical intruders who are troubling first century followers of Jesus. It has been been analysed by Richard Bauckham as follows:

1   Address and greeting (1-2)
2   Occasion and theme (3-4)
3   Background to the appeal: Prophecies of the doom of the ungodly (5-19)
       (a) Three OT types plus interpretation; Michael and the devil
       (b) Three more OT types plus interpretation
       (c) Prophecy of Enoch plus interpretation
       (d) Prophecy of the apostles plus interpretation
4   Appeal (20-23)
5   Closing doxology (24-25)

The Second Letter of Peter is an 'encyclical epistolary epistle' according to N.T. Wright and M.F. Bird. As such it has been been outlined by Richard Bauckham as follows:

1   Address and salutation (1:1-2)
2   Theme: Summary of Peter's message (1:3-11)
3   Occasion: Testament of Peter (1:12-15)
4   Replies to objections: Apostolic witness, value and inspiration of OT prophecy (1:16–21)
5   Peter's prediction of false teachers (2:1-3a)
6   Replies to objections: Certainty of judgement (2:3b-10a)
7   Denunciation of false teachers (2:10b-22)

8   Peter's prediction of scoffers (3:1-4)
9   Replies to objections: Sovereignty of God's word and forbearance of the Lord (3:5-10)
10 Exhortation (3:11-16)
11 Conclusion (3:17-18)

Milieu and Meaning

Jude's author, readers, and date are subject to debate. The letter is attributed to Jude, who appears to be the brother of Jesus (Matthew 13:55; Mark 6:3). A story is told by Eusebius (AD 260-340), Bishop of Caesarea and church historian, citing an earlier writer, that the grandchildren of Jude were interrogated by Domitian, Roman emperor AD 81-96, about their Davidic lineage, their possessions, and the kingdom of Christ. Domitian did not detain them. They exercised authority in the churches of Judea as witnesses and relatives of the Lord until the time of Trajan, Roman emperor AD 98-117. It would be reasonable to say that the letter could have been written by Jude or an admirer between 60 and 90 to readers who were influenced by followers of Jesus in Judea.

The setting of Jude can be explored by examining its opponents, extra-canonical traditions, and Old Testament examples.

Its opponents are attacked in the following manner: *these dreamers also defile the flesh, reject authority, and slander the glorious ones ... these people slander whatever they do not understand, and they are destroyed by those things that, like irrational animals, they know by instinct ... These are blemishes on your love-feasts, while they feast with you without fear, feeding themselves ... These are grumblers and malcontents; they indulge their own lusts; they are bombastic in speech, flattering people to their own advantage ... It is these worldly people, devoid of the Spirit, who are causing divisions.(Jude 8, 10, 12, 16, 19)*

These opponents appear to be antinomian: they *pervert the grace of our God into licentiousness (Jude 4c)*. (Antinomian is another word for lawless.) They may even be proto-gnostic: they *deny our only Master and Lord, Jesus Christ (Jude 4d)*. (Gnostics denied the uniqueness of Jesus.)

Its traditions include quotations from Jewish religious literature:
But when the archangel Michael contended with the devil and disputed about the body of Moses, he did not dare to bring a condemnation of slander against him, but said, 'The Lord rebuke you!' (Jude 9) It was also about these that Enoch, in the seventh generation from Adam, prophesied, saying, 'See, the Lord is coming with tens of thousands of his holy ones, to execute judgement on all, and to convict everyone of all the deeds of ungodliness that they have committed in such an ungodly way, and of all the harsh things that ungodly sinners have spoken against him.' (Jude 14-15)

These traditions are not reproduced in 2 Peter. It seems likely that by the time of 2 Peter these quotations are omitted due to disfavour towards non-canonical books.

Its examples build a strong case to warn the readers against moral laxity and rationalistic thinking.

There are three Old Testament examples: *the Lord, who once for all saved a people out of the land of Egypt, afterwards destroyed those who did not believe ... the angels who ... left their proper dwelling, he has kept in eternal chains ... for the judgement of the great day ... Sodom and Gomorrah ... which ... indulged in sexual immorality ... serve as an example by undergoing a punishment of eternal fire. (Jude 5-7)*

Furthermore, after the references to Michael and Enoch, there are three more Old Testament examples: *Woe to them! For they go the way of Cain, and abandon themselves to Balaam's error for the sake of gain, and perish in Korah's rebellion. (Jude 11)* These examples are re-ordered in 2 Peter.

When Jude 4-18 is compared with 2 Peter 2:1-3:3, it is apparent that there is a literary relationship between Jude and 2 Peter.

Jude	2 Peter
6 *And **the angels** who did not keep their own position, but left their proper dwelling, he has **kept** in eternal chains in **deepest darkness for the judgement of the great day***	2:4 *For if God did not spare **the angels** when they sinned, but cast them into hell and committed them to chains of **deepest darkness** to be **kept until the judgement***

*7 Likewise, **Sodom and Gomorrah** and the surrounding cities, which, in the same manner as they, indulged in sexual immorality and pursued unnatural lust, serve as an example by undergoing a punishment of eternal fire*

*2:6 and if by turning the cities of **Sodom and Gomorrah** to ashes he condemned them to extinction and made them an example of what is coming to the ungodly*

*8 Yet in the same way these dreamers also defile the **flesh**, reject **authority***

*2:10 especially those who indulge their **flesh** in depraved lust, and who despise **authority***

*10 **But these people slander** whatever they do not understand, and they are **destroyed** by those things that, **like irrational animals**, they know by **instinct***

*2:12 **These people, however, are like irrational animals**, mere creatures of **instinct**, born to be caught and killed. They **slander** what they do not understand, and when those creatures are destroyed, they also will be **destroyed***

*11 Woe to them! For they go **the way** of Cain, and abandon themselves to **Balaam**'s error **for the sake of gain**, and perish in Korah's rebellion*

*2:15 They have left the straight road and have gone astray, following **the road of Balaam** son of Bosor, who loved **the wages** of doing wrong*

12-13 *These are blemishes on your love-feasts, while they **feast** with you without fear, feeding themselves. They are **waterless** clouds carried along by the winds ... wandering stars, **for whom the deepest darkness has been reserved** for ever*

2:13, 17 *They are blots and blemishes, revelling in their dissipation while they **feast** with you. These are **waterless** springs and mists driven by a storm; **for them the deepest darkness has been reserved***

16 *These are grumblers and malcontents; they indulge their own **lusts**; they are **bombastic** in speech, flattering people to their own advantage*

2:18 *For they speak **bombastic** nonsense, and with licentious **desires** of the flesh they entice people who have just escaped from those who live in error*

17-18 *But you, **beloved, must remember the predictions of the apostles of** our Lord Jesus Christ; for they said to you, '**In the last** time there will be **scoffers, indulging** their own ungodly **lusts**'*

3:1-3 *... **beloved** ... you **should remember the words spoken in the past** by the holy prophets, and the commandment of **the Lord** and Saviour spoken through your **apostles**. First of all you must understand this, that **in the last** days **scoffers** will come, scoffing and **indulging** their own **lusts***

Is it really possible that the parallels are a coincidence? Is it at all likely that both documents used an earlier source? Is it possible that the shorter Jude is a condensation of the longer 2 Peter? Is it most likely that the earlier Jude is the basis of the later Jude? When all is said and done, the fourth suggestion is most acceptable: Jude 4-18 is utilised by 2 Peter 2:1-3:3.

On the one hand, Jude has traditions from strange Jewish writings in Jude 9, drawn from a story about a dispute between the archangel Michael and the devil about the corpse of Moses, and in Jude 14-15, quoting from the apocryphal book of Enoch about the the coming of the Lord in judgement. As has been noted, it seems likely that by the time of 2 Peter these quotations are omitted due to disfavour towards non-canonical books.

On the other hand, 2 Peter refers to the story of the transfiguration of Jesus in 2 Peter 1:16-18 drawn from traditions enshrined in Matthew and Mark: *but we had been eyewitnesses of his majesty. For he received honour and glory from God the Father when that voice was conveyed to him by the Majestic Glory, saying, 'This is my Son, my Beloved, with whom I am well pleased.' We ourselves heard this voice come from heaven, while we were with him on the holy mountain.*

The letters are probably written before the end of the first century (Jude) and after the beginning of the second century (2 Peter). Jude criticises opponents who are morally lax and somewhat rationalistic. Jude's opponents divorce their beliefs from their morals. Second Peter, which uses Jude as a source, also criticises later opponents for the same reasons. In addition, 2 Peter has another reason for criticising its opponents: their scepticism. They sceptically dismiss the hope of Christ's second coming.

However, there are some straightforward things to be said.

First, both documents testify to Christian communities confronting moral laxity. *For certain intruders have stolen in among you, people who long ago were designated for this condemnation as ungodly, who pervert the grace of our God into licentiousness and deny our only Master and Lord, Jesus Christ. (Jude 4) They promise them freedom, but they themselves are slaves of corruption. (2 Peter 2:19a)*

Second, both documents witness to groups of believers facing rationalistic thinking. *"In the last time there will be scoffers, indulging their own ungodly lusts." It is these worldly people, devoid of the Spirit, who are causing divisions. (Jude 18-19) First of all you must understand this, that in the last days scoffers will come, scoffing and indulging their own lusts and saying, "Where is the promise of his coming? For ever since our ancestors died, all things continue as they were from the beginning of creation!" (2 Peter 3:3-4)*

Third, both Jude and 2 Peter provide remedies for doubt. On the one hand, Jude mentions four positive elements: *Build yourselves up on your most holy faith; pray in the Holy Spirit; keep yourselves in the love of God; look forward to the mercy of our Lord Jesus Christ that leads to eternal life. (Jude 20-21)* Jude also emphasises divine help: *Now to him who is able to keep you from falling, and to make you stand without blemish in the presence of his glory with rejoicing, to the only God our*

Saviour, through Jesus Christ our Lord, be glory, majesty, power, and authority, before all time and now and forever. Amen. (Jude 24-25)

On the other hand, 2 Peter lists helpful qualities: *You must make every effort to support your faith with goodness, and goodness with knowledge, and knowledge with self-control, and self-control with endurance, and endurance with godliness, and godliness with mutual affection, and mutual affection with love. For if these things are yours and are increasing among you, they keep you from being ineffective and unfruitful in the knowledge of our Lord Jesus Christ. (2 Peter 1:5-8)* Second Peter also stresses human growth: *But grow in the grace and knowledge of our Lord and Saviour Jesus Christ. To him be the glory both now and to the day of eternity. Amen. (2 Peter 3:18)*

Mission

Howard Marshall notes four significant themes of Jude:

First, God's judgement upon immoral sinners correlates with his mercy for those who repent.

Second, God and Christ are juxtaposed in judgement and salvation.

Third, the apocalyptic strand in Judaism is utilised by the author.

Fourth, the congregation's role in pastoral care is to care for sinners and those whom they lead astray.

Howard Marshall also notes five significant themes of Second Peter:

First, unusually the transfiguration of Jesus is emphasised as a pointer to his exaltation as Saviour, Lord, and God.

Second, faith is linked with a personal knowledge of Christ.

Third, believers share in the divine nature.

Fourth, a negative verdict is given on the perishable world but it is to be replaced by a new heaven and earth.

Fifth, it is important to hold fast to the apostolic tradition and to understand it correctly.

Jude and 2 Peter are written by two followers of Jesus.

Jude refers to Jesus six times:

*Jude, a servant of **Jesus Christ** ... To those who are called, who are beloved in God the Father and kept safe for **Jesus Christ** ... For certain intruders have stolen in ... who pervert the grace of our God into licentiousness and deny **our only Master and Lord, Jesus Christ** ... But you, beloved, must remember the predictions of the apostles of **our Lord Jesus Christ** ... look forward to the mercy of **our Lord Jesus Christ** that leads to eternal life ... to the only God our Saviour, through **Jesus Christ our Lord**, be glory, majesty, power, and authority ... (Jude 1, 4, 17, 21, 25)*

Second Peter refers to Jesus eight times:

*Simeon Peter, a servant and apostle of **Jesus Christ**, to those who have received a faith as precious as ours through the righteousness of **our God and Saviour Jesus Christ**: May grace and peace be yours in abundance in the knowledge of God and of **Jesus our Lord** ... For if these things are yours and are increasing among you, they keep you from being ineffective and unfruitful in the knowledge of **our Lord Jesus Christ** ... entry into the eternal kingdom of **our Lord and Saviour Jesus Christ** will be richly provided for you ... I know that my death will come soon, as indeed **our Lord Jesus Christ** has made clear to me. For we did not follow cleverly devised myths when we made known to you the power and coming of **our Lord Jesus Christ**, but we had been eyewitnesses of his majesty ... For if, after they have escaped the defilements of the world through the knowledge of **our Lord and Saviour Jesus Christ**, they are again entangled in them and overpowered, the last state has become worse for them than the first ... But grow in the grace and knowledge of **our Lord and Saviour Jesus Christ** ... (2 Peter 1:1, 2, 8, 11, 14, 16; 2:20; 3:18).*

Both documents challenged readers in ancient times with the figure of Jesus.

In the context of competing faiths, mysterious forces of destiny, secret societies, and alternative philosophies, Jude includes three Old Testament types (the people of the Exodus, the fallen angels, Sodom and Gomorrah), a dispute between the archangel Michael and the devil, three more Old Testament types (Cain, Balaam, Korah), a quotation from the book of Enoch, a prediction of the apostles. All of this is before a sevenfold appeal. Fortunately, the closing prayer of praise is readily understandable in the twenty-first century.

In a similar way, 2 Peter replies to a series of objections by harking back to apostolic witness and prophetic message, predicts the rise of false teachers and indulgent scoffers, and denounces them by incorporating much of Jude. Then he stresses the sovereignty of God's word and the forbearance of the Lord. In conclusion, he makes a heartfelt appeal in view of new heavens and a new earth, with a passing reference to the letters of Paul.

But how does one make the transition to the twenty-first century in reading Jude and 2 Peter? Of Jude, Raymond Brown says, 'We owe Jude reverence as a book of Sacred Scripture, but its applicability to ordinary life remains a formidable difficulty.' Of both documents James Dunn is bold enough to ask, 'The question of how much Christianity would have lost if Jude and 2 Peter had not been included in the New Testament canon invites a somewhat embarrassing answer.'

But all is not lost. Both documents can challenge readers in modern times. In the face of today's varieties of religion, we shall find that Jude and 2 Peter have something to say to the world religions of Hinduism, Buddhism, Judaism, and Islam. Furthermore, in a world afflicted by war, racism, poverty, disease, drug abuse, pollution, sexual distortion, and climate change, Jude and 2 Peter have relevance.

Jude appeals to ancient and modern readers in seven ways:

(1) *build yourselves up on your most holy faith*
(2) *pray in the Holy Spirit*
(3) *keep yourselves in the love of God*
(4) *look forward to the mercy of our Lord Jesus Christ*
(5) *have mercy on some who are wavering*
(6) *save others by snatching them out of the fire*
(7) *have mercy on still others with fear (Jude 20-23)*
Jude's benediction remains timeless:

Now to him who is able to keep you from falling, and to make you stand without blemish in the presence of his glory with rejoicing, to the only God our Saviour, through Jesus Christ our Lord, be glory, majesty, power, and authority, before all time and now and for ever. Amen. (Jude 24-25)

This magnificent prayer of praise has a fourfold focus.

First, the only God our Saviour is praised because he is able to guard and keep believers from stumbling or falling and because he is able to present and make believers stand unblemished or without reproach. God does this both here and hereafter.

Second, glory or divine radiance, majesty or divine transcendence, power or divine creativity, and authority or victorious freedom - these attributes are ascribed to the only God our Saviour through Jesus the Christ our Lord, the human face of God.

Third, glory, majesty, power, and authority belong to God before all time, now, and for ever. God's greatness is acknowledged from the beginning to end of history.

Fourth, it seems likely the listeners join the reader in saying 'Amen' at the end of the prayer of praise. 'Amen' is a Greek word from Hebrew and means 'So be it' or 'Let it be'.

Second Peter likewise speaks to ancient and modern readers.

On the one hand, 2 Peter's beginning challenges the readers:
you must make every effort to
support your faith with goodness
and goodness with knowledge
and knowledge with self-control
and self-control with endurance
and endurance with godliness
and godliness with mutual affection
and mutual affection with love
... brothers and sisters be all the more eager to confirm your call and election
... in this way entry into the eternal kingdom ... will be richly provided for you (2 Peter1:5-7, 10-11)

On the other hand, 2 Peter's conclusion is salutary:
*But the day of the Lord will come like a thief, and then the heavens will pass away with a loud noise, and the elements will be dissolved with fire, and the earth and everything that is done on it will be **disclosed**.(2 Peter 3:10)*

[As the commentaries reveal, much ink has been spilt in trying to understand 2 Peter 3:10. The most likely Greek text is *everything ... will be disclosed* (literally *found*). However, traditional English versions have followed a less likely Greek text: *everything .. will be burned up*. If one follows this reading one is misled and mistaken. Second Peter teaches not the destruction of the world but the judgement of the world's inhabitants. As the *REB* translates, *the earth with all that is in it will be brought to judgement.*]

Since all these things are to be dissolved in this way, what sort of people ought you to be in leading lives of holiness and godliness, waiting for and hastening the coming of the day of God, because of which the heavens will be set ablaze and dissolved, and the elements will melt with fire? But, in accordance with his promise, we wait for new heavens and a new earth, where righteousness is at home. Therefore, beloved, while you are waiting for these things, strive to be found by him at peace, without spot or blemish; and regard the patience of our Lord as salvation ... But grow in the grace and knowledge of our Lord and Saviour Jesus Christ. To him be the glory both now and to the day of eternity. Amen. (2 Peter 3:11-15, 18)

Intriguingly, the *NEB* marginal note translated 2 Peter 3:18: *But grow up, by the grace of our Lord and Saviour Jesus Christ, and by knowing him.*

In terms of content, the neglected Jude is a letter of exhortation and the enigmatic 2 Peter an encyclical epistolary epistle. In terms of context and clarification, Jude and 2 Peter confront moral laxity and rationalistic thinking. In terms of connection, they present Jesus as Saviour and Judge.

Two Issues arising from 1 & 2 Peter & Jude

(1) Pseudonymity?

Bruce Metzger delivered his thought provoking Presidential Address about pseudonymity at the annual meeting of the Society of Biblical Literature in October 1971 and it was published in the *JBL* in March 1972. It is worth considering.

Motives of ancient pseudepigraphers included literary forgeries with the desire for financial gain, literary fraud out of pure malice, pseudonymous works out of love and respect, pseudepigraphic writings out of modesty, attribution of speeches famous orators, spurious epistles credited classical authors, mistakes in copying manuscripts, and assignment of anonymous works to famous figures.

People in ancient times reacted negatively to works written supposedly by a famous figure, such as the Revelation to John, the Book of Enoch, the Acts of Paul and Thecla, the Gospel of Peter.

Some modern scholars have responded positively to the idea of pseudonymous authors of the Pastoral Epistles or the Wisdom of Solomon. They see no problem at all.

Other modern scholars have exercised a nuanced approach. For example, Kurt Aland argued that anonymity and pseudonymity of NT books are closely connected. Thus originally anonymous books at a later date had titles and names of authors added, such as the Gospels and the Book of Acts.

Other scholars beg to differ. A distinction may be drawn between secular and religious documents. It has been suggested that heretics began the production of pious forgeries and that orthodox writers adopted the practice of pseudonymity in response.

Metzger admits that scholars are not agreed on the distinction between literary frauds and innocent pseudonymous productions. However, he sees no reason for denying inspiration to a book such as 2 Peter which utilises the name of Simon Peter to speak to second and third generation Christians back to orthodox teaching and practice.

(2) A Petrine School?

Marion Soards offers a stimulating proposal. He follows in the footsteps of the work of Alan Culpepper whose doctoral thesis examined nine traits of an ancient school. Culpepper concluded that there was a Johannine School which produced the Fourth Gospel, the Letters of John, and the Revelation to John.

The nine characteristics were as follows:

(1) The community was a fellowship of disciples;
(2) The community traced its origins to a founder;
(3) The community valued the teachings of the founder;
(4) Members of the community were disciples of the founder;
(5) The community's activities included teaching, learning, studying, and writing;
(6) They observed a communal meal;
(7) They had rules to regulate admission and to retain membership;

(8) They maintained some distance from the rest of society;
(9) They were organised to insure the perpetuity of the community.

Soards also examined 1 Peter, 2 Peter, and Jude for literary similarities and dissimilarites, liturgical elements, use of OT, pseudepigraphical literature, and NT. The hypothesis of a Petrine School remains an intriguing suggestion.

However, it should be noted that the hypothesis has not won the approval of Richard Bauckham in his splendid commentary on Jude and 2 Peter. 'It should be borne in mind that the possible derivation of both letters (1 & 2 Peter) from a Petrine "circle" of Christian leaders in Rome is plausible *only* if the "circle" is *not* considered a "school." ... If both letters derive from a Petrine "circle," the circle cannot be a "school" with a common theology, but simply a circle of colleagues who worked together in the leadership of the Roman church.'

Prayer

Lord, help us
>to build ourselves up on our most holy faith;
>to pray in the Holy Spirit;
>to keep ourselves in your love;
>to look forward to the mercy of our Lord Jesus Christ
>leading to eternal life.

Lord, help us to make every effort to add
>goodness to our faith,
>knowledge to goodness,
>self-control to knowledge,
>endurance to self-control,
>godliness to endurance,
>mutual affection to godliness,
>and love to mutual affection.

So may we grow in the grace and knowledge of our Lord and Saviour Jesus Christ to whom be the glory both now and for all eternity. Amen.

Jude & 2 Peter: Select Bibliography

Bauckham, R.J., *Jude, 2 Peter*
Brosend, W., 'Jude, Letter of,' *NIDB*, 3:440-443
Brown, R.E., *An Introduction to the NT*, 748-772
deSilva, D.A., *An Introduction to the NT*, 767-785
Dunn, J.D.G., *Jesus according to the NT*, 172-174
Dunn, J.D.G., *Neither Jew nor Greek*, 96-103, 729-731
Jobes, K.H,, *Letters to the Church*, 233-263, 353-391
Kelly, J.N.D., *The Epistles of Peter & of Jude*, 223-375
Köstenberger, A.J., *Handbook on Hebrews through Revelation*, 147-168, 203-215
Kümmel, W.G., *Introduction to the NT*, 425-434
Marshall, I.H., *NT Theology Many Witnesses One Gospel*, 660-680
McKnight, S., ' 2 Peter' and 'Jude,' *Eerdmans Commentary on the Bible*, 1504-1511, 1529-1534
Metzger, B.M., 'Literary Forgeries and Canonical Pseudepigrapha,' *JBL*, 91: 3-24 (1972)
Powell, M.A., *Introducing the NT*, 481-491, 509-517
Puskas, C.B., *Hebrews, the General Letters, and Revelation*, 92-114
Richard, E., 'Peter, Second Letter of,' *NIDB*, 4:469-475
Rowston, D.J., 'The Most Neglected Book in the NT,' *NTS*, 21:554-563 (1975)
Rowston, D., *A Bird's Eye View of the Bible*, 220-222
Soards, M.L., '1 Peter, 2 Peter, and Jude as Evidence for a Petrine School,' *ANRW*, 25: 3827-3849 (1988)
Watson, D.F., 'The Letter of Jude,' *NIB*, 12:471-500
Watson, D.F., 'The Second Letter of Peter,' *NIB*, 12:321-361
Wright, N.T. & M.F. Bird, *The NT in Its World*, 730-734, 736-740, 749-755, 756-758, 763-769, 777-783

Cave of Apocalypse, Patmos

Library of Celsus, Ephesus

6 The Three Letters of John
The true God

Overview of John's Letters
(adapted from Raymond Brown)
1 John
Date: After the Gospel of John; about AD 100.
To: Followers of Jesus in the Johannine community who had suffered a schism.
Origin: By a writer in the Johannine tradition, not by the writer of the Gospel.
Unity: Most scholars advocate a unified composition rather than a combination of sources.
Addition: A Latin theological gloss was inserted in 5:6-8 (see NRSV margin) about AD 400.
Outline: 1:1-4   Prologue
        1:5-3:10   God is light and we must walk in light.
        3:11-5:12   Walk as children of God who loved us.
        5:13-21   Conclusion

2 John
Date: About the same time as 1 John; about AD 100.
To: Followers of Jesus in the Johannine community who are threatened by schismatic missionaries.
Origin: By a writer in the Johannine tradition.
Outline: 1-3   Opening formula
        4   Expression of joy.
        5-12   Message
        13   Concluding formula

3 John

Date: After 1 and 2 John; shortly after AD 100.
To: Gaius, a Johannine follower of Jesus and a friend of the elder, because Diotrephes, a leader in a neighbouring community, is unfriendly.
Origin: By a writer in the Johannine tradition.
Outline: 1-2 Opening formula
        3-4 Expression of joy.
        5-14 Message
        15 Concluding formula

Message

The possibilities for the genre of First John include a circular letter, an essay, a sermon, and a commentary on the Gospel of John. Questions of genre lead to explanations of structure.

One of the most influential outlines of the book is by Robert Law. He identified three tests of life in the document between the prologue and the epilogue.

1 Prologue (1:1-4)
2 First cycle of tests: righteousness (1:5-2:6), love (2:7-17) and belief (2:18-28)
3 Second cycle of tests: righteousness (2:29-3:10), love (3:11-24), and belief (1 John 4:1-6)
4 Third cycle of tests: love (4:7-21) and belief (5:1-12)
5 Epilogue (5:13-20)

Another outline is given by the renowned Welsh scholar C.H. Dodd in his helpful commentary:

1. Introduction (1:1-4)
2. What is Christianity? (1:5-2:28)
3. Life in the family of God (2:29-4:12)
4. The certainty of faith (4:13-5:13)
5. Postscript (5:14-21)

A third analysis is in the encyclopaedic commentary of Raymond Brown:

1. Prologue: Reflections on the Prologue to John's Gospel (1:1-4)
2. Part One: God is light and we must live in the light (1:5-3:10)
3. Part Two: Live as children of God who has loved us in Christ (3:11-5:12)
4. Epilogue (5:13-21)

Second John is of similar import to First John but on a smaller scale. Clifton Black offers a worthy outline:
1. Saluting the elect lady and her children (1-3)
2. Requests, benefits, and cautions (4-11)
3. Regrets, hopes, and greetings (12-13)

Third John is about church organisation and concerns the claims of two local congregational leaders. Clifton Black offers a helpful outline:
1. Salutation, prayer, rejoicing (1-4)
2. The elder's recommendations (5-12)
3. Regrets, hopes, and greetings (13-15)

Milieu and Meaning

The traditional identification of the author of the Gospel of John, the Letters of John, and the Book of Revelation as the apostle John is maintained by worthy scholars such as Leon Morris, Stephen Smalley, and Karen Jobes. It starts with an argument that the Gospel was written by someone who was a Jew, from Palestine, an eyewitness, an apostle, and, indeed, the apostle John. This argument was put forth in the nineteenth century by the Bishop of Durham, B.F. Westcott. In the twenty-first century the majority of scholars do not accept the veracity of Westcott's fivefold argument and its extension from the Gospel to the Letters and the Book of Revelation.

Alan Culpepper in *John, the Son of Zebedee: The Life of a Legend* draws the conclusion that the author of the Gospel of John, the elder of the three Letters of John, and the seer of the Book of Revelation are different people. He notes that many would distinguish the writer of the Fourth Gospel from the Beloved Disciple. However, similarities of style and thought between the Gospel and the Letters indicate a close relationship between the Gospel and the Letters. So, it appears likely that the Gospel and the Letters come from a Johannine School of followers of Jesus in Ephesus towards the end of the first Christian century. It is also likely that the Book of Revelation belongs to a circle of seven churches in Asia Minor and originates on the Isle of Patmos off the coast in the Aegean Sea. Although the language of Revelation differs markedly from that of the Gospel and the Letters, there are connections of thought which allow for the likelihood of a Johannine School including Gospel, Letters, and Revelation centred in Ephesus.

In time traditions arose of the last days of John the disciple of the Lord in Ephesus encouraging his followers to love one another and resisting the enemies of truth. Jerome (AD 345-420) tells the story of John of Ephesus in his old age being carried to church having only one sermon to preach: "Little children, love one another." Irenaeus (AD 130-200) tells another story of John the disciple of the Lord when he saw the heretic Cerinthus of the bath house at Ephesus. He rushed out without washing and cried out, "Let us escape, lest the bath should fall while Cerinthus the enemy of the truth is in it." This John is identified by Irenaeus as the Beloved Disciple and the author of Gospel, Letters, and Revelation.

Some years ago in his truly groundbreaking commentary on John C.K. Barrett spelled out another hypothesis. It is possible that John the apostle nicknamed a 'Son of Thunder' left Palestine and settled in Ephesus. He may well have composed writings of an apocalyptic nature. After he died his disciples were left wondering about the second coming of Jesus. One of his disciples incorporated his writings in the Book of Revelation at the end of the life of Domitian about AD 96. Another group of his disciples penned the Letters. Yet another disciple produced the first 20 chapters of the Gospel. In due time the final editor incorporated chapter 21 and included references to the Beloved Disciple in his reworking of the Gospel. By the time of Irenaeus the author of Gospel, Letters, and Revelation is identified as one and the same, John the apostle.

In summary, the three Letters of John are written towards the end of the first century from a Christian influenced by John's Gospel to Christians threatened by divisive teachers. The first letter may be the first commentary on the Gospel of John and may be written to rectify misinterpretation of the Gospel. The second letter is of similar import but on a smaller scale. The third letter is about church organisation and concerns the claims of two local congregational leaders. The first letter is of primary importance. The divisive teachers have probably misread the Gospel of John and have not maintained a balance of morality, love and truth.

Howard Marshall notes six significant elements in the Letters of John:

First, the only appropriate life for God's children who claim to be in the light is the ideal of a sinless life. But there is a paradox. On the one hand, believers do sin but can be forgiven and cleared by confessing their sins. On the other hand, it is asserted that people live in God do not sin.

Second, living in God and being anointed by God are ways of expressing the believers' spiritual union with God.

Third, love for God is expressed in love for one another within the faith community and this love is a matter of action not just words.

Fourth, avoiding false belief, particularly about Jesus having come in the flesh, requires testing statements of people who claim that their prophecies are inspired by the Spirit.

Fifth, prayer can be made confidently to God who will answer.

Sixth, another paradox is that believers are kept from harm by Christ and yet they must ensure that they remain in Christ.

Mission

In the First Letter of John, the writer recalls us to the fundamentals of Christianity. *We declare to you what was from the beginning, what we have heard, what we have seen with our eyes, what we have looked at and touched with our hands, concerning the word of life— this life was revealed, and we have seen it and testify to it, and declare to you the eternal life that was with the Father and was revealed to us—we declare to you what we have seen and heard so that you also may have fellowship with us; and truly our fellowship is with the Father and with his Son Jesus Christ. We are writing these things so that our joy may be complete. (1 John 1:1-4)*

On the basis of these basics, the author applies three tests in three cycles.

First, the false teachers claim to live in the light of God just as the writer does. *This is the message we have heard from him and proclaim to you, that God is light and in him there is no darkness at all. (1 John 1:5)* But the false teachers do not live righteously (1 John 1:5 to 2:6), lovingly (1 John 2:7-17) and believingly (1 John 2:18-28). For example, *Whoever says, "I abide in him," ought to walk just as he walked ... Whoever says, "I am in the light," while hating a brother or sister, is still in the darkness ... No one who denies the Son has the Father; everyone who confesses the Son has the Father also. (1 John 2:6, 9, 23)*

Second, the pseudo believers claim to be children of God even as the writer does. *See what love the Father has given us, that we should be called children of God; and that is what we are. (1 John 3:1a)* But the pseudo believers do not exhibit righteousness (1 John 2:29 to 3:10), love (1 John 3:11-24), and belief (1 John 4:1-6). For example, *Everyone who does what is right is righteous, just as he is righteous ... We know that we have passed from death to life because we love one another. Whoever does not love abides in death ... By this you know the Spirit of God: every spirit that confesses that Jesus Christ has come in the flesh is from God, and every spirit that does not confess Jesus is not from God. (1 John 3:7, 14; 4:2-3a)*

Third, the counterfeit Christians claim to live in the love of God as the writer does. *God is love, and those who abide in love abide in God, and God abides in them. (1 John 4:16b)* But the counterfeit Christians do not meet the tests of love (1 John 4:7-21) and belief (1 John 5:1-12). For example, *Those who say, "I love God," and hate their brothers or sisters, are liars; for those who do not love a brother or sister whom they have seen, cannot love God whom they have not seen ... Those who believe in the Son of God have the testimony in their hearts. Those who do not believe in God have made him a liar by not believing in the testimony that God has given concerning his Son. (1 John 4:20; 5:10)*

In conclusion, the writer says that his readers should get back to basics. *And this is his commandment, that we should believe in the name of his Son Jesus Christ and love one another, just as he has commanded us. All who obey his commandments abide in him, and he abides in them. And by this we know that he abides in us, by the Spirit that he has given us. (1 John 3:23-24)*

Second John is of similar import but on a smaller scale to the First Letter. Third John is about church organisation and concerns the claims of two local congregational leaders.

Peter Rhea Jones (citing T.F. Johnson) notes what God says to believers in 1 John:

1. You are forgiven. *If we confess our sins, he who is faithful and just will forgive us our sins and cleanse us from all unrighteousness.(1:9)*

2. You know God. *Whoever says, 'I have come to know him', but does not obey his commandments, is a liar, and in such a person the truth does not exist; but whoever obeys his word, truly in this person the love of God has reached perfection. By this we may be sure that we are in him: whoever says, 'I abide in him', ought to walk just as he walked.(2:4-6)*

3. You know and belong to the truth. *But you have been anointed by the Holy One, and all of you have knowledge. I write to you, not because you do not know the truth, but because you know it, and you know that no lie comes from the truth ... And by this we will know that we are from the truth and will reassure our hearts before him.(2:20-21; 3:19)*

4. You are the children of God. *See what love the Father has given us, that we should be called children of God; and that is what we are. The reason the world does not know us is that it did not know him. Beloved, we are God's children now; what we will be has not yet been revealed. What we do know is this: when he is revealed, we will be like him, for we will see him as he is... The children of God and the children of the devil are revealed in this way: all who do not do what is right are not from God, nor are those who do not love their brothers and sisters. (3:1-2, 10)*

5. You are loved. *In this is love, not that we loved God but that he loved us and sent his Son to be the atoning sacrifice for our sins. Beloved, since God loved us so much, we also ought to love one another. (4:10-11)*

Peter Rhea Jones also sees four models of ministers in 3 John:

First, Jones warns against being 'Oppositional Diotrephes' (vv.9-10). Such a person 'appears egocentric, reactionary, uncooperative, controlling' among other things.

Second, Jones highlights 'Cooperative Gaius' (vv. 3, 5-7). Gaius is 'a refreshing alternative' to Diotrephes. 'Gaius embodied the best in Johannine Christianity.'

Third, Jones identifies 'the Stalwart Elder' (vv. 1-6, 8-12, 15). The Elder 'was grounded, thought theologically, … was ethically oriented, an advocate of missions, supportive, sensitive to individuals.'

Fourth, Jones spotlights 'Promising Demetrius' (v. 12). Demetrius 'reflects an undeniable integrity of life and faith.'

Prayer

Lord, help us to live in your light. Lord, help us to live as your children. Lord, help us to live in your love. We acknowledge our need to adhere to the basics of consistent righteousness, constant love, and Christian belief. And so we thank you for the blessed assurance of being forgiven, knowing you, belonging to the truth, being your children, experiencing your love. We pray in the name of Jesus who died for us, rose again, and has given us your Spirit. Amen.

The Letters of John: Select Bibliography

Barrett, C.K., *The Gospel according to St John*, 133-134
Black, C.C., 'The First, Second, and Third Letters of John,' *NIB*, 12:363-469
Brown, R.E., *An Introduction to the NT*, 383-405
Brown, R.E., *The Epistles of John*
Culpepper, R.A., *The Gospel and Letters of John*
Culpepper, R.A., *John, the Son of Zebedee: The Life of a Legend*, 307-320
deSilva, D.A., *An Introduction to the NT*, 388-408
Dodd, C.H., *The Johannine Epistles*
Dunn, J.D.G., *Jesus according to the NT*, 167-171
Dunn, J.D.G., *Neither Jew nor Greek*, 103-106, 774-782
Jobes, K.H., *Letters to the Church*, 395-450
Jones, P.R., *1, 2 & 3 John*, 152, 278-279
Köstenberger, A.J., *Handbook on Hebrews through Revelation*, 169-201
Kümmel, W.G., *Introduction to the NT*, 434-452
Law, R., *The Tests of Life*
Marshall, I.H., *NT Theology Many Witnesses One Gospel*, 529-547
Mitchell, M.M., 'John, Letters of,' *NIDB*, 3:370-374
Painter, J., '1, 2, and 3 John,' *Eerdmans Commentary on the Bible*, 1512-1528
Polhill, J.B., 'First, Second, & Third John,' *Mercer Commentary on the Bible*, 1311-1318
Powell, M.A., *Introducing the NT*, 493-507
Puskas, C.B., *Hebrews, the General Letters, and Revelation*, 115-140
Rowston, D., *A Bird's Eye View of the Bible*, 217-220
Wright, N.T. & M.F. Bird, *The NT in Its World*, 784-807

7 The Book of Revelation
The Alpha and the Omega, the first and the last

Overview of Revelation
(adapted from Raymond Brown)

Date: Between AD 92 and 96 at the end of Domitian's rule.
To: Churches in western Asia Minor
Origin: Written by a Jewish Christian prophet named John who was neither the apostle John (Gospel) nor the elder John (Epistles).
Unity:The writer included visions and passages from Christian apocalyptic tradition, but overall the work is entirely his own.
Outline:
1:1-3   Prologue
1:4-3:22   Letters to the Seven Churches
Part I of the Revelatory Experience
4:1-5:14   Visions of the Heavenly Court
6:1-8:1   Seven Seals
8:2-11:19   Seven Trumpets
Part II of the Revelatory Experience
12:1-14:20   Visions of the Dragon, the Beasts, & the Lamb
15:1-16:21   Seven Plagues and Seven Bowls
17:1-19:10   Judgement of Babylon, the Great Harlot
19:11-22:5   Victory of Christ and the End of History
22:6-21   Epilogue

Message

The last book in the Bible can be characterised in three ways: an apocalypse, a prophecy, and an epistle. Consequently, an outline of its contents has to take into account the number, colour, and animal codes of an apocalypse, the forthtelling of God's judgement and mercy of prophecy, and the letters written for publication among the churches.

George Caird (followed by N.T.Wright and M.F. Bird) gives a simple analysis:

I	The prophet's call (1:1-20)
II	The letters to the churches (2:1-3:22)
III	The heavenly council (4:1-5:14)
IV	The seven seals (6:1-8:5)
V	The seven trumpets (8:6-11:19)
VI	The great ordeal (12:1-14:20)
VII	The seven bowls (15:1-16:21)
VIII	The last days of Babylon (17:1-19:4)
IX	The reign of God (19:5-20:15)
X	The new Jerusalem (21:1-22:21)

George Beasley-Murray identifies a prologue (1:1-8) and an epilogue (22:6-21).

James Blevins (following the work of Ernst Lohmeyer and John Wick Bowman) sees Revelation as a drama with seven acts after a prologue and before an epilogue:

Prologue (1:1-8)
ACT I   The seven golden lampstands (1:9-3:22)
ACT II   The seven seals (4:1-8:4)
ACT III   The seven trumpets (8:5-11:18)
ACT IV   The seven tableaux (11:19-15:4)
ACT V   The seven bowls of wrath (15:5-16:21)
ACT VI   The seven judgements (17:1-20:3)
ACT VII   The seven great promises (20:4-22:5)
Epilogue (22:6-21)

My own outline is indebted to the analyses of Caird, Beasley-Murray, Blevins, and Brown. It is as follows:

1:1-8	Introduction: Apocalypse/Prophecy/Epistle
1:9-20	A Vision of Christ: The Son of Man
2:1-3:22	The Seven Lampstands: Ephesus/Smyrna/Pergamum/Thyatira/Sardis/Philadelphia/Laodicea
4:1-5:14	A Vision of Heaven: The Lord and the Lamb
6:1-17; 8:1-5	The Seven Seals: The White Horse/The Red Horse/The Black Horse/The Pale Green Horse/The Martyrs/A Great Earthquake/Prayers of the Saints
7:1-17	Interlude: The Church Militant and Triumphant

8:6-9:21; 11:15-19	The Seven Trumpets: Hail, Fire, Blood/Eruption of a Volcano/ Pollution of Water/Darkness/ Swarms of Locusts/War Horses/Coming of the Kingdom
10:1-11:14	Interlude: Eating the Scroll/Measuring the Temple/ Prophesying by Two Witnesses
12:1-14:5; 14:14-15:4	The Seven Sights: Woman, Child, Dragon/Beast from the Sea/ Beast from the Land/The Lamb and the Church/ The Son of Man/Harvest of Grapes/The Song of the Lamb
14:6-13	Interlude: The Three Angels
15:5-16:21	The Seven Bowls: Curse on the Earth/Curse on the Sea/Curse on the Rivers/Curse on the Sun/Curse on the Throne of the Beast/Curse on the Euphrates/Curse on the Air
17:1-20:3	The Seven Judgements: The Great Whore/The Great City/The Marriage of the Lamb/The Word of God/The Angel in the Sun/The Beast's Defeat/The Devil's Imprisonment
20:4-22:5	The Seven Promises: The Thousand Years/The Judgement of Evil/ New Heaven and New Earth/ Their God and My Children/The Holy City/The Light of the City/ The River of Life
22:6-21	Conclusion: Authenticity/Imminence

Milieu and Meaning

The context of the book of Revelation

The book is written by a prophet named John on the Isle of Patmos towards the end of the reign of Domitian in AD 96. It is directed towards believers in the western area of Asia Minor. Dio Cassius, the Roman historian, says that Domitian moved against 'atheists' in AD 95. Because the Christians denied the reality of the traditional Roman gods, they were accused of atheism. Eusebius, the Christian historian, writes that Domitian 'with his hatred of God and his hostility to him ... proved himself the successor of Nero'. Nero had represented himself on coins as Apollo, god of the sun and son of Jupiter. Domitian goes further by issuing edicts with the words, 'Our Lord and God commands', and by requiring from his citizens the following greeting, 'Hail to the Lord of Lords!'

The codes of the book of Revelation

The writer of the book is a prisoner in a concentration camp on Patmos in the Aegean Sea about 80 kilometres from Ephesus. He writes his book in a secret code to avoid incurring further punishment. The book is then passed around the seven churches on the mainland. He writes to encourage Christians in the face of severe persecution. His secret code is threefold: a number code, a colour code, and an animal code.

Number Code	Colour Code	Animal Code
Fractions =Incompleteness	Pale Green=Death	Frog=Vileness
1=Unity	Dark Green=Life	Eagle=Bad News
2=Witnesses	White=Purity	Beast=Evil
4=Corners of the Earth	Red=War	Beast from the Sea =Caesar
5=Penalty	Black=Famine	Sea Serpent=Satan
6=Imperfection	Gold=Worth	Locusts=Decadence
7=Divine Number	Bronze=Strength	Lamb=Jesus
10=Complete Number	Scarlet=Sin	Lion=Wild Creature
12=Wholeness		Ox=Domesticated Creature

Neither the guards on Patmos nor the Romans in Ephesus understand these codes. When John sends his book to be read aloud in the seven churches, his fellow believers understand the secret codes but their persecutors do not. Consequently, the Christians receive his messages of hope in the midst of suffering. And they do so in safety. After all, some of his secret codes are quite unflattering to the emperor and to the practice of emperor worship.

The category of the book of Revelation

First, the introduction calls the book a revelation (Latin) or an apocalypse (Greek): *The revelation of Jesus Christ, which God gave him to show his servants what must soon take place; he made it known by sending his angel to his servant John, who testified to the word of God and to the testimony of Jesus Christ, even to all that he saw.(Revelation 1:1-2)* With their number, colour and animal codes, revelatory or apocalyptic literature can be likened to political and religious cartoons.

Second, the introduction calls the book a prophecy: *Blessed is the one who reads aloud the words of the prophecy, and blessed are those who hear and who keep what is written in it; for the time is near. (Revelation 1:3)* Prophecy is a forthtelling of God's judgement and mercy.

Third, the introduction calls the book a letter or an epistle: *John to the seven churches that are in Asia: Grace to you and peace from him who is and who was and who is to come, and from the seven spirits who are before his throne, and from Jesus Christ, the faithful witness, the firstborn of the dead, and the ruler of the kings of the earth.(Revelation 1:4-5)* The letters are written for publication among the seven churches of the Roman province of Asia.

The content of the book of Revelation

Like the composer of a symphony, John reworks his themes again and again. By so doing, John emphasises the final victory of God, God's Lamb and God's people over the powers of evil and death.

After the introduction (Revelation 1:1-8), John portrays a vision of Christ (Revelation 1:9-20). Then he transmits letters to seven churches (Revelation 2:1 to 3:22). Next he tells of a vision of the control room at the heavenly headquarters (Revelation 4:1 to 5:14). In the body of the book, John makes his readers stand back to absorb a general impression of God's judgement by means of seals (Revelation 6:1-17; 8:1-5), trumpets (Revelation 8:6 to 9:21; 11:15-19), and bowls (Revelation 15:1 to 16:21).

At times, John takes his readers close up to study the details of God's judgement: 144,000 and countless multitude (Revelation 7:1-17), mighty angel and little scroll (Revelation 10:1-11), two witnesses (Revelation 11:1-14), woman and child (Revelation 12:1-17), two beasts (Revelation 12:18 to 13:18), seven oracles (Revelation 14:1-20).

After the fall of Babylon (Revelation 17:1 to 19:4), John visualises the marriage of the Lamb (Revelation 19:5-10). After the defeat of the beast, the dragon and death (Revelation 19:11 to 20:15), John describes the new creation (Revelation 21:1-8) and the new city (Revelation 21:9 to 22:5).

John's conclusion emphasises the authenticity of his message and the imminence of God's judgement (Revelation 22:6-21).

Themes

According to Howard Marshall a number of theological themes appear in the Book of Revelation:

First, God in heaven decides what is to happen on earth. There is conflict on earth between the followers of Jesus and the world. Powers of evil come down or are cast down from heaven to earth where they deceive and deprave many. The abyss, underneath the earth, is where these powers and those who yield to them are punished.

Second, the main theme of the book is hope which is based on the sovereignty of God who has revealed himself in Jesus.

Third, in the face of oppression experienced by the followers of Jesus God's omnipotence is emphasised. God is ultimately in control of history.

Fourth, the understanding of Jesus is 'second to none' in the NT. The status of Jesus is the Messiah and the Witness.

Fifth, it is possible that the picture of the holy angels surrounding and serving God has been transferred to the Holy Spirit.

Sixth, the forces of evil oppose God and his agents. 'What we might call the beastology of Revelation is as complicated as the angelology.'
Seventh, most importantly, followers of Jesus are to overcome temptation and persecution in a holy resistance.

Finally, God, who brings various judgements upon the world for its evil, is the major actor. Revelation has the common NT belief that the end is near. What was actually near is the sort of human society described by John the Seer including sin and its judgements, the church's witness and its opposition, as well as the church's failures and its reforms. However, the time of the end is unknown.

Mission

Although the word 'hope' does not appear in John's book, the idea is present in his expectation of the future, in his trust in God, and in his patient waiting for God to act. Scattered throughout the book are seven blessings that take us beyond the codes of John to the certainties of Christ.

Blessed is the one who reads aloud the words of the prophecy, and blessed are those who hear and who keep what is written in it; for the time is near ... And I heard a voice from heaven saying, "Write this: Blessed are the dead who from now on die in the Lord." "Yes," says the Spirit, "they will rest from their labours, for their deeds follow them" ... "See, I am coming like a thief! Blessed is the one who stays awake and is clothed, not going about naked and exposed to shame" ... And the angel said to me, "Write this: Blessed are those who are invited to the marriage supper of the Lamb" ... Blessed and holy are those who share in the first resurrection. Over these the second death has no power, but they will be priests of God and of Christ, and they will reign with him a thousand years ... "See, I am coming soon! Blessed is the one who keeps the words of the prophecy of this book" ... Blessed are those who wash their robes, so that they will have the right to the tree of life and may enter the city by the gates. (Revelation 1:3; 14:13; 16:15; 19:9; 20:6; 22:7, 14)

These blessings belong to us in anticipation of the victory of God and his Christ. The triumphant end is certain because it has already begun through God's action in Christ; it is now known through God's presence among his people; and it will be concluded in God's time in the personal presence of Christ amidst the new heavens and the new earth.

Prayer

Lord, we share the hope of all who have read or heard the words of the prophet John. We recognise you as the one who was and is and is to come. Enable us to be among those who live and die as followers of Jesus. We look forward to the celebration of the victory of God and his Christ. Help us to be faithful and true in the certainty of a renewed heaven and a renewed earth which are finally united in Christ the Victor. Amen.

Revelation: Select Bibliography

Beasley-Murray, G.R., *The Book of Revelation*
Blevins, J.L., *Revelation as Drama*
Brown, R.E., *An Introduction to the NT*, 773-813
Caird, G.B., *The Revelation of St John the Divine*
deSilva, D.A., *An Introduction to the NT*, 786-830
Dunn, J.D.G., *Jesus according to the NT*, 175-186
Dunn, J.D.G., *Neither Jew nor Greek*, 106-110, 782-791
Koester, C.R., 'Revelation, Book of,' *NIDB*, 4:785-798
Köstenberger, A.J., *Handbook on Hebrews through Revelation*, 217-266
Kümmel, W.G., *Introduction to the NT*, 452-474
Marshall, I.H., *NT Theology Many Witnesses One Gospel*, 548-566
Powell, M.A., *Introducing the NT*, 519-537
Puskas, C.B., *Hebrews, the General Letters, and Revelation*, 141-164
Reddish, M.G., 'Revelation,' *Mercer Commentary on the Bible*, 1325-1347
Reddish, M.G., *Revelation*
Rowland, C.C., 'The Book of Revelation,' *NIB*, 12:501-743
Rowston, D., *A Bird's Eye View of the Bible*, 227-232
Rowston, D., *Promises and Blessings in the Book of Revelation*
Smalley, S.S., *The Revelation to John*
Wright, N.T. & M.F. Bird, *The NT in Its World*, 808-847

Conclusion

In the preceding pages we have travelled from the Unread (Hebrews) to the Misread (Revelation). After looking at the world of the New Testament, we have examined the Message, Milieu, Meaning, and Mission of each document from Hebrews to Revelation. In the process I trust that we have been challenged to ask questions and find answers about the content, the context, the purpose, the reason, the connections of each document. In other words, we have thought about the "then and now" of these neglected writings of the New Testament.

Tom Long, the great American preacher. in his book *Shepherds and Bathrobes* mentions a theological student approaching a great theologian who had just lectured on the authority of the Bible. The student was clutching in his hand a large black leather-bound Bible. The student raised his voice and asked the theologian, 'Do you believe that this is the Word of God?' The theologian looked at the student's fingers tightly gripping the Bible. 'Not if you think that you can grasp it,' said he. 'Only when the Bible grasps you.'

It is my hope that readers of these books in the New Testament will have the experience of the Bible grasping them. This will happen when they meet Jesus in the pages of the documents from Hebrews to Revelation. At the age of thirteen I was baptised in a suburban church in Melbourne and promised to follow Jesus. As a student in secondary school, university, theological college, and theological seminary I learned to read the Bible spiritually and academically. Since then as a theological lecturer, a religious education teacher, a local church pastor, and an adjunct lecturer it has been my privilege and responsibility to share the message of the Bible.

In the ups and downs of life I continue to be grasped by the Bible as I meet Jesus as *the pioneer and perfecter of our faith* (Hebrews), *our glorious Lord Jesus Christ* (James), *the shepherd and guardian of your souls* (1 Peter), *our only Master and Lord* (Jude), *our Lord and Saviour* (2 Peter), *the true God* (1 John), and *the Alpha and the Omega, the first and the last* (Revelation). May this be the experience of the readers of *From Unread to Misread*.

Finally, a prayer of Søren Kierkegaard (1813-1855), who valued religious experience, seems appropriate at the end of our journey from the Unread (Hebrews) to the Misread (Revelation):

O Lord Jesus Christ, I love to live in your presence, to see your human form and to watch you walking on earth. I do not want to see you through the darkened glass of tradition, nor through the eyes of today's values and prejudices. I want to see you as you were, as you are, and as you always will be. I want to see you as an offence to human pride, as a man of humility, walking among the lowliest of men and women, and yet as the saviour and redeemer of the human race. Amen.

Annotated Bibliography

Of making many books there is no end ...(Ecclesiastes 12:12)

Eerdmans Commentary on the Bible (Wm. B. Eerdmans Publishing Co., 2003)
An excellent one volume commentary on the Bible. Note contributions on Jude and 2 Peter.

Mercer Commentary on the Bible (Mercer University Press, 1995)
Another excellent one volume commentary on the Bible. Note contributions on Hebrews, James, 1 & 2 & 3 John, and Revelation.

New Interpreter's Bible Vol. 12 (Abingdon Press, 1998)
Introduction, Commentary, and Reflections on each document from Hebrews to Revelation.

New Interpreter's Dictionary of the Bible 5 Vols.(Abingdon Press, 2006-2009)
See each chapter's select bibliography for relevant articles.

Barrett, C.K., *The Gospel according to St. John* (Westminster Press, 1978)
A superb commentary by the finest British commentator on the NT in the 20th century.

Bauckham, Richard J., *Jude, 2 Peter* (Word Books, 1983)
The most comprehensive commentary on two neglected NT books.

Beasley-Murray, G.R., *The Book of Revelation* (Oliphants, 1974)
A most useful commentary on the most misread book in the NT by an outstanding Baptist scholar.

Blevins, James L., *Revelation as Drama* (Broadman Press, 1984)
A gifted scholar's interpretation of the Book of Revelation in terms of Greek drama.

Brown, Raymond E., *An Introduction to the New Testament* (Doubleday, 1997)
A user friendly NT introduction by the leading American Catholic NT scholar of the 20th century. There is an abridged edition edited by Marion L. Soards published by Yale University Press, 2016.

Brown, Raymond E., *The Epistles of John* (Doubleday, 1982)
The most comprehensive commentary on the Johannine Epistles.

Bruce, F.F., 'To the Hebrews' or 'To the Essenes'? *New Testament Studies*, 9:217-232 (1963)
An examination of the hypothesis that Hebrews was written to members of the Qumran community.

Bruce, F.F., *New Testament History: The Jews, The Romans, And The Church* (Kingsley Books, 2018)
A reprint of Bruce's excellent historical survey first published in 1982.

Bruce, F.F., *The Epistle to the Hebrews* (Wm. B. Eerdmans Publishing Co., 1990)
A revised edition of the best English commentary on Hebrews for general use.

Buechner, Frederick, *Beyond Words* (HarperSanFrancisco, 2004)
A simply marvellous collection of wry, witty, and wise reflections on sacred and ordinary words a well as biblical characters.

Caird, G.B., *The Revelation of St John the Divine* (A. & C. Black, 1966)
A truly insightful commentary by an influential NT scholar.

Culpepper, R.Alan, *The Gospel and Letters of John* (Abingdon Press, 1998)
A succinct introduction and commentary on the Gospel and Letters by a skilled interpreter.

Culpepper, R.Alan, *John, the Son of Zebedee: The Life of a Legend* (T&T Clark, 2000)
A comprehensive study of the images of the Apostle John throughout Christian history.

deSilva, David A., *An Introduction to the New Testament Contexts, Methods & Ministry Formation* Second Edition (IVP Academic, 2018)
A beautifully presented NT introduction with excellent treatment of exegetical skills and cultural awareness.

Dodd, C.H., *The Johannine Epistles* (Hodder & Stoughton, 1946)
A timeless masterpiece by the Welsh doyen of NT scholars.

Dunn, James D.G., *Beginning from Jerusalem* (Wm. B. Eerdmans Publishing Co., 2009)
An all-encompassing history of the Christian faith from AD 30 to 70 by the Scottish NT scholar. .

Dunn, James D.G., *Neither Jew nor Greek* (Wm. B. Eerdmans Publishing Co., 2015)
A comprehensive history of the Christian literature from AD 70 to 200.

Dunn, James D.G., *Jesus according to the New Testament* (Wm. B. Eerdmans Publishing Co., 2019)
A helpful survey of the NT witnesses to the figure of Jesus.

Filson, Floyd V., *'Yesterday'* (SCM Press, 1967)
As the subtitle says, a study of Hebrews in the light of chapter 13.

Jobes, Karen H., *Letters to the Church* (Zondervan, 2011)
An attractive introduction to the NT books Hebrews to Jude from a conservative viewpoint.

Jones, Peter Rhea, *1, 2 & 3 John* (Smyth & Helwys, 2009)
A superb commentary which bridges the gap between the academy and the church.

Kelly, J.N.D., *The Epistles of Peter & of Jude* (Harper & Row, 1969)
A fine commentary by the Oxford Patristics scholar.

Köstenberger, Andreas J., *Handbook on Hebrews through Revelation* (Baker Academic, 2020)
A reading of the NT books Hebrews to Revelation from a completely traditional perspective.

Kümmel, Werner Georg, *Introduction to the New Testament* (Abingdon Press, 1975)
An erudite NT introduction for advanced readers.

Law, Robert, *The Tests of Life, a Study of the First Epistle of St. John* (T&T Clark, 1909)
The classic study of 1 John as an apparatus of tests.

Long, Thomas G., *Hebrews: Interpretation* (John Knox Press, 1997)
A study of the sort of sermon preached in the earliest Christian churches.

Marshall, I. Howard, *New Testament Theology Many Witnesses One Gospel* (IVP Academic, 2004)
An examination of NT Theology as missionary theology. There is an abridged edition *A Concise New Testament Theology* (IVP Academic, 2008).

Martin, Ralph P., *James* (Word Books, 1988)
A commentary in the pattern of the Word Biblical Commentary: Translation, Form/Structure/Setting, Comment, Explanation.

Metzger, Bruce M., 'Literary Forgeries and Canonical Pseudepigrapha,' *Journal of Biblical Literature, 91: 3-24 (1972)*
A most insightful study of pseudonymity.

Moody, Dale, *The Word of Truth* (Wm. B. Eerdmans Publishing Co., 1981)
A legendary Baptist theologian's summary of Christian doctrine based on biblical revelation.

Montefiore, Hugh W., *The Epistle to the Hebrews* (A. & C. Black, 1964)
A useful commentary based on the hypothesis that the author was Apollos.

Moule, C.F.D., 'The Nature and Purpose of I Peter,' *New Testament Studies*, 3:1-11 (1956)
An examination of the suggestion that a baptismal sermon is applied to a situation of persecution.

Powell, Mark Alan, *Introducing the New Testament: A Historical, Literary, and Theological Survey* Second Edition (Baker Academic, 2018)
A very accessible and most attractive presentation of the NT writings.

Puskas, Charles B., *Hebrews, the General Letters, and Revelation* (Cascade Books, 2016)
A reading of the NT books Hebrews to Revelation from a historical critical perspective.

Reddish, Mitchell G., *Revelation* (Smyth & Helwys, 2001)
A most readable and an extremely helpful commentary.

Rowston, Douglas J., 'The Most Neglected Book in the New Testament,' *New Testament Studies*, 21:554-563 (1975)
A summary of a doctoral dissertation examining Jude's opponents, resources, apostolicity, setting, and impact.

Rowston, Doug, *A Bird's Eye View of the Bible* Second Edition (MediaCom, 2014)
A user-friendly approach to reading through the Bible as a single story of God and his relationship with his creation.

Rowston, Doug, *Promises and Blessings in the Book of Revelation* (Morning Star Publishing, 2015)
A study of the seven promises to the faithful followers of Jesus and the seven blessings for the readers of the Revelation to John.

Selwyn, E.G., *The First Epistle of St Peter* (Macmillan, 1946)
A truly classical commentary on the Greek text advocating the importance of Silvanus as Peter's scribe in Rome.

Smalley, Stephen S., *The Revelation to John* (IVP Academic, 2005)
A comprehensive commentary based on the hypothesis that the author was the apostle John in the reign of Vespasian.

Soards, Marion L., '1 Peter, 2 Peter, and Jude as Evidence for a Petrine School,' *Aufstieg und Niedergang der Römischen Welt [Rise and decline of the Roman world]*, 25: 3827-3849 (Walter de Gruyter & Co., 1988)
A stimulating proposal of a Petrine School behind 1 Peter, 2 Peter, and Jude.

Wright, N.T. & Michael F. Bird, *The New Testament in Its World* (SPCK/Zondervan, 2019)
Bird's redaction of Wright's distinctive contributions to the study of the NT including reading the NT, the NT world, Jesus, the resurrection, Paul, the Gospels, early Christian writings, the NT text and canon, and the NT for today. Simply brilliant.

www.ingramcontent.com/pod-product-compliance
Lightning Source LLC
Chambersburg PA
CBHW030302010526
44107CB00053B/1783